May It Plea$e the Court

Richard Baldwin Cook

May It Plea$e the Court

First Edition 2009

Copyright Richard Baldwin Cook

ISBN-13: 978-0-9791257-3-7

Nativabooks.com

Nativa LLC
Cockeysville, MD

Available at On Line booksellers & Bookstores
Available also as an e-book, through Amazon.com and elsewhere

Other books by Richard Baldwin Cook include:

That's What I'm Talking About
All of the Above I
All of the Above II

A graduate of Union Theological Seminary in New York and Loyola Law School in New Orleans, Cook's previously published work includes peer reviewed articles and book reviews.

CONTENTS

i

"To produce a mighty book, you must choose a mighty theme. No great and enduring volume can ever be written on the flea."

Herman Melville
Chapter CIV
Moby Dick

Despite Melville's warning, I have a
flea for my subject.
A set of them.

RBC

INTRODUCTION

I pray you, in your letters
When you shall these unlucky deeds relate
Speak of me as I am
Nothing extenuate
Nor set down aught in malice

Nor set down aught in malice. Shakespeare gave (Act V, sc 2) these words to Othello. Murderer though he was, Othello hoped for a true relating of his misdeeds. Is that asking too much?

During the past three years, I have been deprived of my license to practice law in three states. The basis for these official actions against me, the gravamen (in lawyer talk) of my transgressions, was my denunciation of a federal judge for misconduct. The judge's serious misbehavior was ignored by supervising judges. Meanwhile, so-called misconduct was found in my having filed recusal motions and a confidential complaint to those supervising judges. My court filings were met with (1) heavy fines by the subject judge; (2) my suspension from the lawsuit in which I represented several dozen incarcerated women, seeking to remedy the terrible conditions of their confinement; (3) the dismissal, without any investigation, of my confidential complaints to the supervising judges and (4) Formal Charges brought against me, years later, by a Disciplinary Counsel, in the employ of state court judges, many of whom accept gifts from lawyers who appear before them. According to a Formal Complaint, my misconduct "centered" on one of my recusal motions and my confidential complaint about the judge. (See pages 37, 177, below.)

3

I resisted as aggressively as I knew how. I submitted responses to the Formal Charges, and also submitted numerous of my earlier pleadings. I questioned the jurisdiction of the disciplinary proceedings because the rules precluded the examination of the conduct of the judge – the very essence of my defense. I asked that my complaints about the judge be forwarded to a US attorney. All to no avail. In three states my license to practice law has been "suspended" for a period of time. I find myself the misbegotten subject of judicial orders, perpetually designating me an unethical attorney. Meanwhile, no one ever disputed the truthfulness of the statements I made about the conduct of the judge. No one can dispute them. He did what I said he did.

This book is my attempt at redress. Six chapters deal with the proceedings which led to my condemnation and removal from the practice roles in three states. (Two states ratified what had been done after I had been through a hearing in the first state. I could have asked for separate hearings in these two states, but why? A Disciplinary Counsel (DC) will not consider complaints of misconduct about the actions of a judge. I was kicked to the curb for making *allegations* even though an examination would show the allegations were *true*. The DC of state No 2 concluded I should not be prosecuted but prosecuted me anyway after state No. 1 did so. The DC of state No 3 declined to answer my detailed letter outlining events, which vindicated me and incriminated the federal judge. Rather than investigate or even respond to me, this DC transferred the file to an associate DC, who pretended I had never answered the charges.)

The seventh chapter is my assessment of the federal Code of Judicial Conduct, which has recently been revised. The revisers are lawyers and judges, who stand to gain financially from the giving of gifts to judges and the reciprocal beneficial rulings, which flow back from the bench to the gift-givers. Chapter eight offers a silver of hope for a solution to this mess.

Like Othello, I believe it is dishonorable that something be set down against me in malice. In truth, I did what they said I did. *I denounced a judge for accepting gifts and for doing a favor in return.* I do not believe I should have suffered any degree of professional sanction for this.

The Decree of the state Supreme Court depriving me of my license to practice law is a public document. It has been published by the Court and has appeared on the Web. In this book, the Court's decision is discussed and criticized line by line. I have placed the court's Order in *italics*. The parts I comment on are highlighted in both *italics* and **bold type**.

All personal references and place identifications have been deleted – even when I have quoted from the Court's own published decision. The deleted material has been replaced by [IDD] – for *identity deleted* - even though the state Supreme Court's own Order identifies by name the persons who figure in the proceedings. I have taken this precaution out of a fear of further proceedings against me. I no longer dream of doing any good for anyone as an attorney but I do, still, have an occasional nightmare about further dealings with these be-robed hooligans and the hucksters who gift them with money. NOTE: The Court's Decision is attached at the end of this book, as an Appendix.

5

It is dangerous to leave written that which is badly written. A chance word, on paper, may destroy the world. Watch carefully and erase, while the power is still yours.

William Carlos Williams
Patterson
Book 3, Part III

CHAPTER I

DEALERS NOT USERS

A state Supreme Court ought not to have charged me with professional misconduct without investigating the serious, factual charges of wrongdoing, which I had first made against a United States District Judge. The state court should not have found it preferable to remove me from the legal profession without first determining what, if anything, ought to have been done about the judge. In the event (as far as I know), nothing was done.

My complaints of judicial misconduct were treated as mere *allegations* and never investigated by judicial authorities, charged with supervising the conduct of members of the judiciary. My statements of fact (see pp. 85-99, below) about the judge's actions were ignored by the judges who condemned me. Because supervising judges have disregarded their duty to get to the bottom of complaints of judicial misdeeds, I have refrained from mentioning by name anyone whose actions are mentioned in this narrative. Let the judiciary complete now what they have avoided up to now.

I suppose I could mention by name anyone who has already been publicly identified by a state's high court. But I confess to a lingering anxiety in naming names, in light of the sloppy and incomplete examination given these matters by the be-robed custodians of legal and judicial ethics. In disciplining me, the judges did not hesitate to

7

employ innuendo and inference, even though a straightforward, impartial investigation was asked for and was obviously called for. My ordeal demonstrates that the state disciplinary counsel is not after the facts – but is there to protect the regime of gift-giving to the judges.

There is no statement I have made regarding any of the matters taken up here, which is not the truth and which was not supported either by documents or by the statements of third parties. Anyone who reads relevant files in the federal District Court, the Judicial Council or the state Supreme Court will know this to be the case.

SUPREME COURT OF [IDD]
NO. [IDD]
IN RE: RICHARD B. COOK
ATTORNEY DISCIPLINARY PROCEEDINGS

*This disciplinary matter arises from formal charges filed by the Office of Disciplinary Counsel ("ODC") against respondent, Richard B. Cook, an attorney **licensed to practice law** in [IDD].*

With the first sentence, we run into a statement that falls somewhere short of the truth. I was NOT licensed to practice law in [IDD] at the time of the disciplinary proceedings in 2004. Having moved to another state and passed that state's Bar, I had placed my earlier [IDD] law license in inactive status. My only active law license was in my new state of residence.

In exercising authority to regulate lawyers, every state's highest court uniformly forbids non-lawyers from practicing law; to practice, an active license or a waiver of some kind is required. A person who possesses only an inactive license normally must associate with a practitioner with a currently active license. Serious misconduct must be in prospect for a state's highest court to reach out to discipline, and publicly humiliate, an individual with only an inactive law license.

Part of the problem with the case against me was that several years had passed before I was formally charged with any ethical offense related to my work in the lawsuit. A delay of years between the the filing of formal charges is, in itself, a kind of on-going punishment. Confronted by a delayed disciplinary inquiry, one hesitates to undertake any new legal work. There is a fear that, years later, a charge will be filed; at that moment, a judge, opposing counsel and new client(s) all would need to be notified about pending charges of misconduct. This development would, of course, destroy the value of that new, un-related representation. Such a revelation might even open the door to a charge of malpractice by a client, who was only just then told of a "problem" years before. With an investigation hanging over me for years, before any charges were filed against me, I never felt I should take a new client and never did. The delay was not due to an investigation of the charges I had made against my judge; no investigation has every occurred.

In ordering the suspension of my law license, the state Supreme Court stated that it had reviewed the record so as to be sure things had been done fairly and properly. From the Decision, here is the language of the Court:

. . . we act as triers of fact and **conduct an independent review** *of the record to determine*

whether the alleged misconduct has been proven by **clear and convincing evidence***.*

It is important for the reader to know at the outset that the Supreme Court of [IDD] takes upon itself the burden of assuring fairness in disciplinary proceedings and discharges this burden by reviewing "the record" created by the hearing committee and the disciplinary board. Presumably, this "record" includes all of the pleadings and documents submitted to these subordinate entities. If not, one would have to re-submit every item at every stage. Here is the text of the Decision, with my comments:

UNDERLYING FACTS

In November 1996, respondent began representing the plaintiffs in a civil matter captioned [IDD], Judge [IDD], presiding (hereinafter referred to as [IDD]). The plaintiffs in [IDD] were a group of female prison inmates who alleged their civil rights were violated as a result of physical and sexual abuse at the hands of their prison guards.
On June 26, 1998, respondent filed a motion in [IDD] in which he **implied** *that the court had improperly never "permitted representative civil rights plaintiffs to proceed as class representatives." He also* **implied** *that Judge [IDD] had improperly met with and dissuaded a local attorney from enrolling as co-counsel for the plaintiffs.*

He implied . . . he also implied – I was plaintiffs' counsel for five years. In the course of those five years, dozens of pleadings were filed and orders issued. In its selection from five years of litigation, the state Supreme Court focuses attention on a handful of pleadings, which are taken to be "underlying facts" and (*by implication only*) taken to have been improperly filed. Curiously, the Court raises but then declines to answer the questions posed by the pleadings the Court itself has selected and characterized as mere *implications*:

- Had my judge ever permitted civil rights litigants to proceed as representatives of the class of prisoners?
- did my judge improperly meet with and dissuade a local attorney from enrolling as co-counsel for the plaintiffs?

Why is it professional misconduct even to inquire of a court about these two matters? When these questions were placed before him, my judge refused to answer them, as did, in their turn, the Justices of the state Supreme Court.

The five-year litigation background and the immediate context for these inquiries are simply ignored by the Justices. I had asked for class certification for the 90-100 plaintiffs (approximately ½ of the population of the prison), whom I had interviewed and who had signed representation agreements with me.

I had also requested a class certification hearing for the plaintiffs. To bolster this motion, I had employed a physician and asked her to review several dozen statements from prisoners and also prisoner medical records and she had prepared a report, which was submitted to the court. The Justices of the state Supreme Court have taken no notice of my futile attempts to obtain class certification, including the contents of the medical report, or any of the other submissions I made.

For his part, my judge denied the motion(s) for class certification. The state Supreme Court, finding misconduct on my part, has simply ignored my question to the Judge: has he *ever* certified a class action lawsuit? Ever? I had been told by an attorney from the ACLU National Prison Project that prisoner class action lawsuits were unwelcomed in this court and in this particular Federal Circuit, generally.

It should not be considered professional misconduct to bring a court's past conduct before that very court. Why is it unethical to inquire of a judge if a theoretical remedy available under federal law is, in practice, not permitted to incarcerated women in this federal district court? The state Supreme Court cited no authority, state or federal, for the proposition that it is improper to raise the questions I raised with the federal judge.

My request(s) for a hearing for class certification were denied. Under then controlling federal court authority, a denial of class certification absent a hearing is frowned upon. The state Supreme Court either did not know of this controlling federal authority or did not care. The Justices were content to cite my motions as evidence of some kind of unspecified misconduct, without noting my attempts, over months and years, to establish my clients' eligibility to proceed as a class.

To bring suit as representatives of a class, plaintiffs who prevail are unlikely to receive any significant compensation. The remedy they seek is a *change in conditions for the class.* To their great credit, all of my 90-100 clients – incarcerated, abused women - knew this and had agreed to proceed as a class of plaintiffs, rather than as individual plaintiffs.

Just as the state Supreme Court ignored federal precedent, which favors a hearing prior to denial of class certification, the Justices also ignored a duty to explain how it is misconduct to ask a federal judge if he has *ever* certified a class of plaintiffs. In finding my question unethical *per se,* the Justices do not bother to notice how my Judge answered the question: he simply ignored it. Apparently, there are some questions that cannot be asked in federal court – such as: have any plaintiffs before this court ever been accorded the privilege to seek remedies for similarly situated persons? Such a forbidden question will not only be ignored; if you raise it, you can expect to be driven from the legal profession.

I was over forty years old when I went to law school. My life experience had included arrests for civil disobedience and subsequent confrontations in court with one or two judges, who were inclined to overlook the freedoms of speech and assembly. I had not learned then and did not learn in law school that properly filed recusal motions and confidential complaints about judicial misconduct will cost you your career. The one true rule, not the misleading judicial complaint ritual is what counts: in the presence of miscreant ROBED AUTHORITY, you are supposed to whinny and break into a trot.

Prior to the loss of my law licenses, I assumed the rules governing judicial ethics meant something. I also believed that, as an officer of the court, I was entrusted with a degree of responsibility to see that these rules were not breached to the

13

detriment of my clients. Looking back, I cannot imagine why I ever thought that.

*. . . He also **implied** that Judge [IDD] had improperly met with and dissuaded a local attorney from enrolling as co-counsel for the plaintiffs.*

implied - More misconduct on my part – but only because the Court ignores the fact that I had provided the name and date when a lawyer had met with the Judge, and a transcript of his phone call to me confirming this meeting. The Justices of the state Supreme Court stay on their chosen route of innuendo and shadowy misstatements. Because the actual facts are against a finding of misconduct, the facts are ignored.

My Judge *did meet* with a local lawyer, who from that moment forward, *refused* to communicate with me. My repeated phone calls to him were never acknowledged or returned. (See pp. 100, 126.) The state Supreme Court Justices knew this - if they actually read the record of the case, as they said they did. The meeting took place. The only question is: did my Judge dissuade this young attorney from joining to represent the plaintiffs? I asked the Judge about this. He refused even to acknowledge the question. The question itself is then trotted out by the state Justices as my further misconduct.

As with all questions, there is a context to my question about whether the judge had interfered with my efforts to secure local counsel. I had moved out of state after this lawsuit was filed and was interested in obtaining local counsel. I needed local help. Litigating from long distance was expensive and frustrating. In the course of the lawsuit, the court permitted the defendant jailers, to turn me away from the prison if I arrived unannounced and wanted to speak with a prisoner. On more than one occasion, I made a 1,000 mile trip to central [IDD] from my residence, asked to speak with XX or YY prisoner, and was denied access. Even though XX and YY had communicated with me, I was still blocked from speaking with them, as per orders of the court. The orders blocking me from speaking with prisoners were routinely given orally, by the Magistrate Judge, who was called by counsel for the jail to complain that the jail had no prior notice of my desire to speak with XX or with YY. These orders were issued over the phone. Sometimes I received these "orders" in a phone booth near the prison.

Neither the Court nor the Justices of the [IDD] Supreme Court have taken the trouble to explain – or to cite a precedent – for the theory that plaintiffs' counsel must first obtain the permission of a defendant before interviewing a witness.

I was not charged with misconduct for asking specific questions of my judge. Best not, concluded the custodians of attorney discipline, file a formal charge for raising awkward questions. Somebody might expect answers. An innuendo alleging misconduct is good enough, in a proceeding that is not subject to normal prosecutorial guidelines. A straightforward look for facts might trigger an inquiry into the judge's conduct. This kind of proceeding might make a conviction of a lawyer difficult to obtain, if the lawyer's only failing was having asked questions, whose answers might prove embarrassing.

An attorney disciplinary matter is not a typical prosecution. A garden variety prosecution, in theory, is subject to constitutional protections

15

(rights), which benefit the subject of the prosecution. These *rights* include access to evidence and to witnesses prior to a formal hearing. Things are different for a lawyer, who is made the subject of an ethical complaint. This lawyer finds himself subjected to what the judges call a *quasi-prosecution*. In a mushy quasi-prosecution, the rules and the procedures are weighted heavily against the accused.

As I discovered, (1) vague innuendos, (2) reliance entirely upon witnesses who were either adverse to me in other litigation or employed by the judge I complained about, and (3) a distorted and incomplete narrative of events selected from six years of litigation, is good enough to sustain a conviction. The point of all this was to banish me from the legal profession, not to find the truth – since bringing truth into the light of day would have been uncomfortable for a federal judge.

In the state where I was prosecuted for misconduct, the disciplinary counsel who brings a charge of lawyer misconduct is granted sweeping investigative powers, which the accused lawyer cannot utilize in his defense. Before charges are filed, the disciplinary counsel may, on demand, examine any documents and interview anyone. After the filing of formal charges and at all times for the accused lawyer, a court order must be sought and (hopefully) obtained before documents or a reluctant witness may be examined. By rule, the disciplinary proceedings are not to be delayed while such court supervision is sought.

These absurdly unfair procedures are intended not to uncover truth but rather to facilitate a conviction. From 1,000 miles away, I could only seek documents or witness testimony by applying

16

to, and appearing before, a state judge in [IDD] – knowing all the while that the *quasi-prosecution* of me would go forward and I might be confronted with additional charges of delay if the disciplinary proceedings against me got mired down.

Pressing a federal judge to explain why he had interfered with my efforts to obtain local counsel became evidence of serious misconduct, worthy of the public suspension of my (inactive) license to practice law. Meanwhile, the rationale for my urgent reason for the need for local help was simply ignored. The Justices who prosecuted me lacked the simple honesty to acknowledge that the federal court itself had interfered with my efforts to represent my clients by blocking my attempts to interview witnesses at a prison.

Unannounced visits to a prison being sued by the prisoners are obviously important. If the jail knows in advance who is a potential witness against the jail, there is ample opportunity for pressure, threats, transfers, and violence to be directed against inmates. Even before suit was filed, a number of women inmates had been moved two hours away from the jail on the eve of an announced visit. In addition, several women prisoners had signed statements saying they had been threatened or physically abused by jailers, as soon as the prison had been informed of their desire to speak with an attorney. The state Supreme Court Justices knew this – assuming they had read the files of the case, as they said they did.

My conclusion is this. In its published Opinion, removing me from the roll of licensed attorneys, the state Supreme Court was signaling to lawyers licensed under its supervision: *don't ever try to ask a judge if he has engaged in misconduct.*

The Court continued its recitation of salient "underlying facts."

On December 31, 1998, respondent filed a motion entitled "Plaintiff's Response to the State Defendants' Motion to Dismiss Certain Plaintiffs." In this motion, respondent stated that if Judge [IDD] granted the defendants' motion, then "the courts in the [IDD] can be reserved almost entirely for wealthy (predominantly white) litigants, and courts and counsel need not be concerned with poor (predominantly black) plaintiffs." He also **claimed** *that Judge [IDD] compounded the "lack of balance" between the plaintiffs' resources and the defendants' resources through his "unwritten orders, his failure to respond to plaintiff motions, [and] his refusal to even place this case on the docket for many months at the outset." Finally, respondent suggested that this case would not end until "either the plaintiffs prevail or the Court concludes that the rape and abuse of inmates by their guards is perfectly OK."*

The State Supreme Court cites certain of my pleadings, which are of concern to it, but does not indicate how or why any of the pleadings are evidence for a finding of attorney misconduct. Nor does the Court find it a significant "underlying fact" that my clients - dozens of incarcerated women - had given me sworn statements, which I had previously submitted to the district court, in which they specified the details of their past and continuing abuse in the prison. I wanted this abuse to end. I wanted to identify the responsible parties and protect my clients from them. I concluded during the litigation, stated then and believe today,

18

this Judge's conduct signaled that in his court, "the rape and abuse of inmates by their guards is perfectly OK." I do not regret having told the Judge this and having offered remedies for the horrible situation my clients found themselves in. But I am so disappointed that, as a lawyer, I could do nothing about it. That a state Supreme Court would strike me from the attorney rolls for comments directed at protecting imprisoned women from rape by their guards says more about the kind of judicial slight-of-hand awaiting imprisoned, abused women then it does about my qualifications as a lawyer.

*On January 11, 1999, respondent filed a motion in which he requested that **the following subjects** be discussed at a status conference: 1) the delay in placing the [IDD] case on the docket; 2) reconsideration of the denial of the plaintiffs' class representation; 3) the failure of the court to place one of the plaintiffs' motions on the docket; 4) whether the court has ever authorized class representation in civil rights claims; 5) whether there is a consensus in the court to never allow these types of cases to go forward with class representatives; 6) why Judge [IDD]'s unwritten orders have never been put in writing; 7) whether Judge [IDD] met with a local attorney and dissuaded him from enrolling as co-counsel for the plaintiffs; 8) whether Judge [IDD] has ever appointed counsel to represent an incarcerated person who has complained about conditions of confinement; and 9) whether the court as a whole has ever allowed such a plaintiff to get beyond a defendant's summary judgment or other motion dismissing the complaint.*

The State Supreme Court specifies nine items, which I had wished to discuss with opposing counsel and with the judge. Nowhere in its decision, does the Supreme Court indicate why any of these subjects were improperly raised. Once again, the message is: *do NOT expect the Judge to be made accountable for bias and for mishandling a lawsuit, to the great injury of already defenseless plaintiffs, held within the total control of the defendants.*

The Court continues its identification of "underlying facts."

*On January 14, 1999, respondent filed a motion to recuse Judge [IDD]. The **basis for his motion was his belief** that his clients' opportunity for a fair trial was "slipping away" due to Judge [IDD]'s conduct in the [IDD] case as well as in the case of [IDD] (hereinafter referred to as ["IDD"]. Respondent **alleged** that one of the attorneys in the [IDD] case was Judge [IDD]'s former law partner and the president of an organization that paid for the judge's overseas trip to speak at its conference while the [IDD] case was pending before him. Thereafter, **the case was settled in favor of this attorney's client**. As such, respondent **alleged** that "the judge permitted this counsel's client to benefit from his judicial function." Furthermore, because of the judge's **alleged** conduct in [IDD], respondent argued that the judge "has not maintained the necessary firewall between his personal and his judicial relations and ought not hear Constitutional matters." Regarding the judge's conduct in [IDD], respondent argued that he acted improperly in* *denying the plaintiffs' motion for class representation without conducting a hearing, failed to notice one of the plaintiffs' motions for a hearing, and twice issued oral orders without later putting them in writing. Respondent also accused Judge [IDD] of engaging in "lax case management" and having an "indifference to propriety." He also argued that Judge [IDD] "has not met the judicial requirement of an avoidance of impropriety and the appearance of bias and partiality." Based on these reasons, respondent argued Judge [IDD] should be recused. Judge [IDD] denied the motion to recuse on January 20, 1999, stating that respondent included **only vague allegations** that did not identify a conflict the judge has with the [IDD] case.*

This is a mischaracterization of a properly filed motion, asking a federal judge to transfer a lawsuit to another court. Why mischaracterize what I actually did? Because the State Supreme Court prefers to assert that my "belief" in something or other was "the basis" for my motion of recusal.

The basis for the recusal motion was not a *belief* of mine. No. The basis for the recusal motion and a second recusal motion and also for my *confidential* complaints about the Judge was not some vague notion but rather, a *set of facts*, which I had uncovered:

1. My judge had accepted a significant gift from an organization whose president was a former law partner of the judge and was, at the time the gift was made, simultaneously litigating a matter before this judge;

2. My judge violated the rules of his own court (the Federal Rules of Civil Procedure) by granting a motion by his former law partner to amend a complaint, without first permitting the adverse party to respond or to participate in a hearing on the merits of the motion to amend;

3. My judge was in a real estate partnership, through which he was the landlord of his former law firm - while serving as a United Stated District Judge. The ownership issue was disputed by the law firm, while admitting that papers filed with the Secretary of State of [IDD] showed this judge as an owner. The State Supreme Court took no notice of this factual dispute and thus did not need to resolve it. The only *fact* that concerned the Supreme Court was my having raised this issue as an *allegation*; the Court does not bother to determine if the allegation was *true*.

The Supreme Court decision, which ushered me out of the legal profession, repeatedly characterized my assertions as *allegations*. An allegation is a statement awaiting an inquiry into its truthfulness. No inquiry ever occurred as to my *allegations* about the judge. This permitted the Court to state, repeatedly, that my charges against the judge were never more than allegations - not necessarily the truth. Yet, my statements could also then be taken as evidence of attorney misconduct. With this rhetorical shuffle, the Court avoided both an investigation into the truth of my allegations and any acknowledgment of *judicial misconduct*.

By treating allegations I had made against my judge as if they were false but without establishing their actual falsity, the Supreme Court frees itself to make a career-ending decision as to my eligibility to practice law. By failing to get to the bottom of statements they characterize as allegations, the Justices of the State Supreme Court raised the issue of integrity. They have placed a question mark over their own integrity – not mine.

The statements I made to my judge are factual. They are not merely *allegations*; as specified in my recusal motion, I pointed out:

a. one of the attorneys in the [IDD] case was the Judge's former law partner and the president of a lawyers' organization that paid for the judge's overseas trip while the that case was pending before him.

b. this Judge granted this attorney's motion to amend a complaint without permitting opposing counsel to be heard in opposition – a violation of procedural rules.

c. This case then settled in favor of this attorney's client, thus permitting the judge's former law partner, as I asserted, to benefit from his "judicial function."

What was the "judicial function" about which I complained? The State Supreme Court does not say, although I did. As the Justices of the State Supreme Court knew when they banished me, my complaint about my judge was not because another case had settled. The judicial misconduct was that my judge had forced a settlement upon parties in his court by granting a motion to amend a plaintiff's complaint on the eve of trial and in contravention of procedural rules, which required the opposing party to be heard before a complaint could be amended.

Here is what happened in the other case which alarmed me so greatly that I wanted another judge for my impoverished clients. A motion to amend the complaint was filed before the judge, over the objection of adverse parties. The next day (!) the judge granted this motion. Then applicable Local procedural rules required that, objection to the filing of an amended complaint having been made, *a hearing on the matter must be set.* My judge simply ignored this rule of his own court. Furthermore, Rule 15(a) of the Federal Rules of Procedure, while permitting a court to grant leave to amend a complaint, had been interpreted by the Supreme Court to require a district court to consider "bad faith" [. . .] "dilatory motive" [. . .] "prejudice to the opposing party" before granted leave to amend a complaint. Foman v. Davis, 371 U.S. 178, 182 (1962). Of course, these issues will never be raised if the motion is granted before opposing counsel is heard.

Why would the judge do what he did? The law firm benefitting from the judge's ruling was housed in a building that, according to reports filed with the state Secretary of State, was part-owned by the judge, while he was on the federal bench. After this came to light, a representative of the lessee law firm asserted that an *oversight* accounted for the formal listing, for many years, of Judge [IDD] as a part owner of the property after he became a federal judge. The fact of ownership may be in legitimate dispute. If so, the dispute could have been settled by examining the business records of the law firm and the financial records of the judge. I asked for these records – after the Federal Circuit Judicial Council did nothing. For this, I was subjected to severe penalties – imposed by the subject judge – for making this request.

Before formal charges were filed against me, I asked that the Disciplinary Counsel (DC) examine these records. This request was ignored. This meant there was no pressure on the Justices (who employ the DC and who took away my law license) to acknowledge that I could not have engaged in bad faith in stating that the judge was the owner of a building housing a law office. No bad faith on my part or any other improper purpose could have been demonstrated, since I was relying on documents furnished by the judge's former law firm and formally filed in the office of the Secretary of State. But a concession that no bad faith could be found in my citing of official documents would have undermined the case against me, to say nothing of the obvious implication that someone ought to get to the bottom of an ownership interest involving a federal judge. The Justices were not about to go there. It was far easier and more convenient for them to throw away the career of an officer of their own court than to examine the business and personal financial records of an active federal judge and those lawyers the judge:

- is in business with
- was in business with
- no longer is in business with.

Well, fact-finding Justices, which is it?

What had happened in this court – which the Justices of the state Supreme Court refuse to look into – is that a last-minute, improper grant of leave to amend a lawsuit had led directly to a crushing defeat for one set of litigants and an overwhelming victory for the judge's former partners (and his apparent renters). His granting of leave to amend made the defendants *personally* liable for their *official* conduct. I was not permitted to do so, but someday someone must look into this lawsuit, in which hundreds of thousands of dollars went to a plaintiff and plaintiff's counsel – the judge's buddies – after the judge permitted their complaint to be amended outside the controlling procedural rules. (I am going to go way out on a limb here and speculate that the costs of domestic and overseas trips for some of the judges on the Federal Circuit and also on the state Supreme Court are footed by folks with an interest in the outcome of court business – including the same attorneys who gifted my judge.)

About this debacle of a lawsuit, only so much is known. What is not known remains unknown because supervising judges, who are responsible for the ethical behavior of a district judge refused to look further into the matter, after I complained. What is known is this: the attorney who brought the motion to amend the Complaint was a former law partner and declared real estate partner of the Judge. Following the amendment, the case settled for $1.7 million. The local newspaper reported that "most" of the $1.1 million portion of the settlement paid by an insurance company would go to this attorney's law firm – the judge's former law firm, which paid rent on a building part-owned (according to formally filed documents) by the judge. I complained about this and lost my law license for doing so.

These shenanigans by my judge – permitting a complaint to be amended in violation of the procedural rules – apparently netted hundreds of thousands of dollars for his former law firm. If the law firm does not see big paydays, it may have trouble paying the landlord(s) their rent. And by the way, how much is the rent? Who are/were the other real estate partners? How are the landlords paid? The State Supreme Court, finding misconduct on my part for merely raising such questions, is not interested in answering them. Is this because state court judges *also* have business ties to litigators in their courts? Is the prevalence of these arrangements the reason why it was decided to send a message to the bar by removing me from the practice of law?

My judge's actual conduct was the basis for my confidential judicial complaint. Specification of this conduct as well as the surrounding circumstances are to be found (1) in pleadings I filed before the Judge, and (2) in complaints I made to the Federal Circuit Judicial Council, and (3) in the files of the disciplinary proceedings which were instituted against me. None of this background was worthy of the attention of the State Supreme Court, as part of its recitation of important "underlying facts." The justices were content to throw away my reputation as an ethical person and my career as a lawyer because I had complained to a United States District Judge and to his supervising judges, about his venal, documented misconduct.

By stating that all I had to complain about was my *belief* and some vague notions about a court's *judicial function,* my reputation as an ethical lawyer could be trashed. The Justices need not acknowledge the judicial misconduct, which I complained about: the court forced a settlement beneficial to the judge's personal friends (and, according to formally filed ownership records) to himself as a landlord, by improperly flaunting the procedural rules of his own court.

By ignoring the actual, factual, truthful basis for my complaints of misconduct by the federal judge, the state Supreme Court's characterization of my federal court pleadings is false and misleading. And final, career-ending, in its finality. Additional assertions of mine apparently were so shocking to the Justices, that they found it impossible to investigate them; it was sufficient to condemn me – for stating truthfully:

- this federal judge did not maintain "the necessary firewall between his personal and his judicial relations"

- this federal judge acted improperly in denying the plaintiffs' motion for class representation without conducting a hearing

- this federal judge "failed to notice one of the plaintiffs' motions for a hearing, and twice issued oral orders without later putting them in writing"

- this federal judge engaged in lax case management and was guilty of "indifference to propriety."

- this federal judge in fact had "not met the judicial requirement of an avoidance of impropriety and the appearance of bias and partiality."

All of this was not merely alleged. It was true. My judge did everything I said that he did. In an inquiry resulting in the blackening of my professional reputation, none of this mattered, because a duty to the truth was not recognized by the justices of the State Supreme Court. Merely referencing a lawyer's complaints about a judge, declining to examine the complaints for their truthfulness, hurrying on, instead, to the finding of misconduct – all of this amounts to an absurd and harsh indifference to the truth of what I had stated in formal pleadings and in *confidential* complaints to supervising judges.

When it comes to enforcing ethical standards or even in matters of truth-telling, these federal circuit court judges and state Supreme Court justices are dealers, not users.

MANNY, YOU DON'T KNOW OUR JUDGES

A lie always harms another; if not some particular man, still it harms mankind generally, for it vitiates the source of law itself. [. . .] Whoever tells a lie, however well intentioned he might be, must answer for the consequences, however unforeseeable they were, and pay the penalty for them even in a civil tribunal. This is because truthfulness is a duty which must be regarded as the ground of all duties based on contract, and the laws of these duties would be rendered uncertain and useless if even the least exception to them were admitted. To be truthful (honest) in all declarations, therefore, is a sacred and absolutely commanding decree of reason, limited to no expediency.

Immanuel Kant, "On a Supposed Right to Lie from Altruistic Motives," *The Critique of Practical Reason* (Univ of Chicago, 1949, pp. 346-50).

If for I want that glib and oily art,
To speak and purpose not;
since what I well intend,
I'll do't before I speak,
--that you make known.
It is no vicious blot, murder,
or foulness,
No unchaste action,
or dishonour'd step,
That hath deprived me
of your grace and favour;
But even for want of that
for which I am richer,
A still-soliciting eye,
and such a tongue
As I am glad I have not,
though not to have it
Hath lost me in your liking.

King Lear
Act One, Scene One

CHAPTER II

FACT ~~FINDING~~ AVOIDANCE

The District Judge's findings of contumacious misconduct by me – which were accompanied by severe monetary sanctions against me – were characterized with approval by the State Supreme Court. Why? The Justices, without measuring my statements for their truthfulness, held that my motion(s) for recusal contained "only vague allegations that did not identify a conflict the judge has with the [IDD] case." I insist: my statements were true. All of them. Each one of them. By condemning my truthful statements, the State Justices have engaged in their own untruth.

Isn't prior, documented misconduct by a judge relevant to his entire docket? If I have discovered a judge has ignored procedural rules so as to favor one party over another and further discover there is a financial interest which might account for this maneuver, I will strenuously object to his presiding over my client's matter. In fact, I think any lawyer has an obligation to do this and risk the consequences. (At least, I thought this, before I discovered how supervising judges handle complaints about judicial misconduct. See Chapter VII.)

- If you know a judge has engaged in misconduct in another matter, why must you stand there in front of him and pretend you do not know it? If you know a valet has stolen someone else's car, should you give him your car keys?

- Is a lawyer to be barred from telling a judge that he believes the judge's misconduct is causing his client's matter to be "slipping away?" No; the lawyer is supposed to protect the interests of his clients at all hazards, and certainly in the courtroom.

- A lawyer is obligated to come forward where there is evidence of judicial misconduct. The appropriate means of coming forward are spelled out in the rules of professional and judicial conduct: file a confidential complaint and/or file a motion of recusal. You are supposed to tell someone. But the revised Rules make a mockery of the notion of fair treatment to a judicial complainant. (Chapter VII, below.)

- Was it true that an attorney in another lawsuit was my judge's former law partner and the president of an organization that paid for the judge's overseas trip, while the case was pending before him? Yes.

- Was it true, then, that my judge had (as I stated) "not met the judicial requirement of an avoidance of impropriety and the appearance of bias and partiality?" Yes.

Nevertheless, the State High Court marches on (**emphasis** added):

*Respondent also filed a [**confidential!**] complaint against Judge [IDD] with the United States Court* *of Appeals for the [IDD] Circuit based on the [IDD] allegations in his motion to recuse. **The [IDD] Circuit dismissed the complaint** on February 2, 1999, stating "[b]ecause Judge [IDD] was not acting improperly either in presiding over a suit in which his former partner appeared as counsel, or in attending the conference, Judge [IDD] is not subject to discipline for the combination of the two." On February 10, 1999, Judge [IDD] provided **detailed** reasons for his denial of respondent's motion to recuse. Essentially, Judge [IDD] ruled that the motion to recuse was frivolous and **cited** the [IDD] Circuit's [**confidential!**] dismissal of respondent's judicial complaint in support of the denial of the motion.*

The [Federal] Circuit dismissed the complaint – The State Supreme Court misleads the reader by stating that "the [IDD] Circuit dismissed the complaint." In fact, it was not a routine panel of judges of the Federal Circuit that made a ruling in a garden variety appeal. It was the *Federal Circuit Judicial Council*, acting as supervising judges. This distinction is crucial because all of the proceedings associated with the Judicial Council are *confidential*. It is inconvenient for the State Supreme Court to point this out – because the Justices then might be expected to explain how this confidential complaint reached the light of day. (In further misconduct, my judge published the Judicial Council decision. See pages 35, 50, 78, 87.) The Justices might also then need to explain how a *confidential* complaint of judicial misconduct can become grounds for a formal and very public charge of misconduct by the lawyer who had made a confidential complaint about a judge.

I am hesitant to quote from my confidential complaint(s) to the Judicial Council or to cite their response(s) because of a lingering requirement of confidentiality. By invoking a confidential ruling of the Federal Circuit Judicial Council, without identifying it as such, and then selectively citing its reasoning and its findings, the Justices placed me at an untenable disadvantage. I cannot respond by quoting statements made by the Judicial Council. This is as unfair to me as it is typical of the state Supreme Court Decision in this matter, which destroyed my reputation while ignoring facts, which demonstrate the judicial misconduct, about which I had initially, and properly, complained.

Once again, we are confronted by a wink from the bench while an incomplete statement is spoken out of the side of the judicial mouth. Not only does the State Supreme Court fail to identify the Judicial Council, even while selectively quoting from its decision, the Court avoids stating that my complaint about my judge, made to the Judicial Council was confidential. It had to be confidential. Those are the rules. *No one* is supposed to make public a confidential judicial complaint without first obtaining approval to do so.

Ignoring the rules of confidentiality, which were as binding upon him as on any other party, my judge publicly identified me as a complainant. He did this by attaching the Judicial Council decision to his order sanctioning me for my recusal motion. He also wrote that the decision of the Judicial Council "bolstered" his own decision to sanction me in the amount of $7,500, for asking him to recuse himself from a lawsuit. (This monetary penalty, plus additional penalties assessed against me by this judge effectively bankrupted my solo law practice – which was doubtless part of this judge's intent.)

There appear to be good reasons for confidentiality about complaints made about a judge. A judge (any judge) is protected from public notice of complaints which might be frivolous. At the same time, a complainant is protected from (possibly) unwanted public attention for having evidence of ethical impropriety by a United States District Judge.

One venue in which it is essential that confidentiality not be breeched is in the very situation that arose in my clients' lawsuit, in which a litigator has evidence of an impropriety and comes forward, confidentially, with the evidence, to supervising judges. By making public my identity as a judicial complainant, my judge destroyed any hope of my clients' settling this lawsuit with the remaining defendants. (Some had already settled – another fact the State Supreme Court finds it convenient to ignore, since the justices intend later in their decision [read on] to state that my conduct had hindered any settlement of the lawsuit.)

There was a reason why settlement with the remaining defendants suddenly was impossible. That reason was that the judge about whom I had filed a confidential complaint had published my identity as a judicial complainant. Why should the defendants settle after being told – by the judge himself – that the plaintiffs' counsel's (truthful) complaint about the Judge's misconduct had been dismissed by the Judicial Council? Armed with this information, why should the other side ever settle? All they have to do is lie in the weeds, waiting for this judge to deal with me. That is exactly what happened.

The "underlying facts" selected by the state Supreme Court Justices include excerpts from the decision of the Federal Circuit Judicial Council, which dismissed my complaint. Why not then quote from my *confidential* complaint? If my reputation and qualifications as a lawyer are at issue, why not cite what I actually said to the Judicial Council? Why not place on the public record, the statements I made, which were the basis for my complaints about my judge's ethical lapses? To do so would raise the obvious question: *why were none of these fact-based complaints ever investigated before I was found to have improperly made them?*

The State Supreme Court, in its Decision, characterizes my judge as providing "detailed" reasons why my recusal motions could be characterized as "frivolous." But some of the issues ignored by the State Supreme Court are these:

- Did my judge acknowledge or deny my statements that the record of another case provided documented evidence of his bias in favor of his friends? He did neither.
- Did my judge explain why he ignored the rules of his own court by deciding a matter related to his financial dealings with lawyers appearing before him? No.
- Did my judge's so-called "detailed" decision include his reasons why he did not refer this matter to another judge, as the rules require? No.
- Did the State Supreme Court or its own agency, the Disciplinary Council, ever investigate my complaints about my judge? No.
- Did the State Disciplinary Counsel refer this matter to a United States attorney, as I asked be

done, before charges were filed against me? No. Was this request even acknowledged? No.

The state Supreme Court found it more convenient to destroy the reputation of any officer of their own court than to investigate his actual, truthful statements. Their alternative was to risk having to conclude that the integrity of the federal judiciary itself is, in this instance, like the Emperor's clothes, notable for its absence.

Let me be clear: I was prosecuted for having made a confidential complaint about a United States District Judge. The April 30, 2004, "Formal Charges" contains (page 2) this statement (**emphasis** added):

Your above detailed conduct constituting harassing and vexatious litigation **centered around** *your January 19, 1999 Motion to Recuse Judge [IDD], the judge assigned to this case; and* **your complaint against Judge [IDD]** *which you filed with the U.S. Court of Appeals, [IDD] Circuit, on February 4, 1999, under docket Number [IDD].*

Centered around – Grave fault was found with conduct that "centered around" something or other. But why not quote my lying accusations? Why not append them to the Court's decision for the world to say and then condemn their terrible aspect? Why not publish the false statements I wrote? Is it because what I wrote was simply the naked truth, a truth the justices prefer to clothe in innuendo?

your complaint against Judge [IDD] – The reader will note that even in the formal charge, care is taken not to identify my offense as a confidential submission to the Federal Circuit Judicial Council. Ought a *confidential* complaint against a federal judge ever become grounds for disciplinary action? Sure. If the objective is to discourage the filing of complaints against judges.

A TRICKED UP JURISDICTION

I should not have been dragged into a disciplinary proceeding under state court jurisdiction for having made truthful complaints about a United State District Judge. Nor should I have been found guilty of misconduct before my complaints were thoroughly investigated. Among the myriad reasons (cited above and below), why the proceedings against me were fundamentally unfair, this point requires emphasis: *attorney disciplinary proceedings lack the jurisdictional authority to review the conduct of a sitting judge.*

Judges (not lawyers) have placed themselves in charge of attorney discipline. It is not surprising, then, to discover that judges have exempted themselves and their conduct from scrutiny under these rules. To his amazement, a lawyer who is to be subjected to discipline for complaining about the misbehavior of a judge, will find out that the prosecutorial authority that has targeted him lacks the power to get to the bottom of the judge's (mis)conduct.

Then-applicable Section 6 C of the State Rules for Lawyer Disciplinary Enforcement stated *"Full-time incumbent judges shall not be subject to the jurisdiction of the lawyer disciplinary agency."* Now, if the disciplinary agency, established and supervised by judges, lacks the authority to review and get to the bottom of my complaints of my

Judge's misconduct, how can I defend myself against the charge that my complaints about a judge were improper? Since the condemning authority is content with characterizations of my actual words while ignoring the words themselves, how can I answer the merely implied criticism that I was not telling the truth? My objection about improper jurisdiction was brought up at the outset of the proceedings, even before charges against me were filed. These objections were not answered but merely ignored.

My earlier charges entailed assertions that *other lawyers* had engaged in misconduct by gifting my Judge. Did the Disciplinary Counsel look into the conduct of other lawyers? Well, no. Not as far as I know. Prior to the filing of Formal Charges, I urged the Disciplinary Counsel to examine business and tax records of *lawyers and their businesses* with whom my Judge has or had a partnership interest. I also urged that my complaints about my Judge's financial ties to these attorney's be referred to a United States Attorney, who would have had the authority to investigate every aspect of this matter.

These requests were not so much as acknowledged by the Disciplinary Counsel, the agent and employee of a State Supreme Court. What are they afraid they might find? That an investigation into the gifting of this particular federal judge, might shine an indirect and very unwelcome light on business and financial ties between litigators in lower state courts supervised by these particular Justices? That such shenanigans are not uncommon in the Justices' own court? Disciplinary proceedings against an attorney ought not become a shield against inquiries into the gifting of judges, who then do favors in return.

MONEY-TO-ME / RULING-FOR-YOU

Why would a lawyer such as myself, residing out of state, in solo practice, with only an inactive law license, be publicly humiliated by state court judges, for bringing truthful complaints, which entailed the likely misconduct of other lawyers and the blatant misconduct of a sitting United States District Judge? The obvious reason is to send a message: don't criticize a judge for taking a gift and for doing return favors for his pals and business associates. The underlying reality is that judges simply do not discipline each other for financial improprieties involving money they obtain from lawyers. Nor do judges discipline lawyers for giving them money. Instead, Justices of a state's highest court will punish a lawyer who complains – even confidentially to supervising judges – about these financial arrangements.

I believe that lawyers, working through various attorney associations, routinely send judges on expensive domestic and overseas trips. If so, then these lawyers obviously benefit when the gifted judge bends the procedural rules in their favor. Having been removed from the legal profession, I have discovered that the money-to-me / ruling-for-you two-step gets a wink and a nod from other judges, who do not want to close that spigot. Before expecting the members of a state's highest court to green light an investigation into gift-giving attorneys, one would want to know if these justices themselves have been sent travelling, with costs footed by attorneys, or attorney associations. Might a look into this practice dig up a spigot – or even an underground torrent? But who's gonna dig? Not the judges. They knock the trowel out of your hand.

The State Supreme Court, working backward from its finding of my culpability, carries its heavy rhetorical load uphill toward the pre-determined goal – guilty as charged:

On February 22, 1999, respondent filed a second complaint against Judge [IDD] with the [IDD] Circuit based on Judge [IDD]'s **reference** *to the [IDD] Circuit's dismissal of respondent's first judicial complaint, thereby publishing the fact that respondent was a judicial complainant. The complaint was also based on an* **allegation** *that Judge [IDD] had a financial interest in the building housing his former law firm, one of whose partners was representing a party in a case before Judge [IDD]. The [IDD] Circuit* **dismissed** *this complaint on May 12, 1999.*

The questions just leap off the page.

1. Where is the text of my complaint?
2. Did it contain true statements?
3. Is the mere filing of a complaint against a United States District Judge, grounds for suspension from the practice of law?
4. Is the content of my complaint just terrible enough to become the basis for a suspension, but too terrible to quote from?
5. On what basis was the complaint "dismissed" by the Judicial Council? Was the Council's reasoning cogent or mistaken?
6. What were the specific facts alleged in this confidential complaint? Were these allegations determined to be false? Frivolous? Irrelevant? Burdensome? Abusive? Redundant? Reckless? Obnoxious? Or, perhaps . . . truthful?

7. Did (do?) the Circuit Judges also receive travel gifts from these self-same lawyers? From any lawyers? From an association of lawyers? From the self-same lawyers' association I complained about?

None of this is worthy of inquiry by the State Supreme Court. Better simply to destroy the reputation of a lonely, lowly lawyer, in solo practice, residing out of state and possessing an inactive State law license – who foolishly fails to follow the pay-to-play rules, and is too impolite to keep his mouth shut, when his judge is caught playing pay-to-play with some other lawyers.

Isn't it the case that a complaint placed before the Judicial Counsel must be kept confidential? Yes. That is the case. Then, what does the State Supreme Court make of its own statement, that a federal Judge made a "reference" to the Federal Circuit's dismissal of my judicial complaint – a complaint made confidentially? By publishing the Judicial Council's decision, the judge, who was the subject of the complaint, undermined my ability to effectively represent my clients before that very judge. This brazen abuse of judicial power receives not a hint of concern from the Justices, whose minds are focused elsewhere: let's just bury this particular lawyer. *Rest in Peace, Counselor. And your complaint of judicial misconduct can lie there, dead, beside you.*

The state Supreme Court fudges the actual facts. Even their reference to the "reference" is a dodge. My judge did not simply make a "reference" to the Federal Circuit Judicial Council decision; he appended it to his sanction order, dismissing my recusal motion. The Supreme Court is compelled to acknowledge that my judge made public that I had filed a complaint against him. But the Justices select the most neutral word available for this rule violation; my Judge, according to the State Supreme Court, makes but a "reference." That is a little bit like saying Hitler made a "reference" to Jews once in a while.

The State Supreme Court just cannot bring itself to state forthrightly what my judge actually did and to state honestly that his conduct was improper. One suspects, if this had been admitted, the entire proceeding against me would have collapsed around the Justices' ears. What I had said was: a United States District Judge had engaged in judicial improprieties. Had the State Supreme Court at any point acknowledged this, then two questions would have come up: (1) *why is the Court punishing a lawyer for coming forward to object to obvious, documented, judicial misconduct?* And (2) *why didn't the judges on the Federal Circuit Judicial Council do something about this Judge?*

Reading the mind of the Justices, I suggest there is a short answer to both questions: *we must join the Federal Circuit judges in protecting a venal and vindictive federal district judge against truthful complaints because, if we do not, we will be shutting off our own $$ spigot.*

The findings of "facts" continue:

*In April 1999, respondent filed **a second motion to recuse** Judge [IDD] in the [IDD] case.*

a second motion to recuse - The charges against me make no mention of fault having been found with a second recusal motion. But, never mind. I am still subject to condemnation for having

43

brought it. In a *quasi prosecution*, there is no need to amend a complaint. And no need to worry about procedural unfairness, in condemning conduct that was not ever formally cited as *mis*conduct. A lawyer mired in murky disciplinary proceedings can answer a complaint in detail, as I did – and then discover that the Ruling condemning you will cite as misconduct matters that had not been brought up before the Ruling was written.

The motion was based on Judge [IDD] making public the fact that respondent had filed a judicial complaint against him with the [IDD] Circuit. Judge [IDD] denied the motion on May 6, 1999.

What is one to make of this narrative? My judge violated the Judicial Complaint Rules of the Federal Circuit by flouting the confidentiality requirements contained in those rules. This misconduct, all by itself, destroyed my ability to adequately represent my dozens of clients. Since the Judicial Council did nothing about this deliberate violation of its own rules, then, neither will the offending Judge and neither will, in their turn, the State Supreme Court.

One hesitates to imagine the consequences that await a lawyer or a member of the public, who violates the mandate of confidentiality found in the Judicial Complaint Rules. But the Judge who (1) has engaged in obvious misconduct and who (2) himself violates the rules intended to assure the public that members of the judiciary are engaging in proper conduct – such a judge is not required to comply with the rules. The sad and simple truth is this: when it comes to the conduct of a judge, who is the subject of a complaint made under the judicial complaint rules, there are no rules. And no worry, judge; the supervising judges have got your back.

By sanctioning me for coming forward with truthful complaints about judicial misconduct, the Justices of a State Supreme Court are winking at the sorry ethical mess in the federal courts. The Justices need not have ventured into this thicket. By pursuing public, formal charges of misconduct against me, the disciplinary counsel (DC), creature of the state Supreme Court, could have simply acknowledged an obvious jurisdictional problem - state disciplinary procedures vs. federal judge misconduct – and declined to act. Or the DC could have conducted an honest investigation before filing charges. The DC did neither. When it was their turn, the Justices committed their own serious mistakes. Their procedural peccadilloes led them into substantive errors. They crafted a Decision, which is essentially a series of false and misleading statements, designed to conceal the federal judge's misconduct, which they and the DC knew had occurred.

They ought to be ashamed of themselves. These custodians of the ethics of the legal profession had a complete set of pleadings, which pointed to a truthful narrative about judicial misconduct, which should have required a different outcome – vindication of an officer of their own court. They ignored all to protect the miscreant federal judge.

More from the Decision, with **emphasis** added:

*Thereafter, in an attempt to further investigate his **allegations** regarding Judge [IDD]'s improprieties in other cases, including the [IDD] case, respondent sought to take the deposition of*

45

[IDD], the former office manager of Judge [IDD]'s former law firm, [IDD], and its real estate partner, [IDD]. However, **neither [IDD] were parties to the [IDD] case; thus, Judge [IDD] quashed the deposition.** *Respondent* **also sought to subpoena documents** *from [IDD]. Both filed objections to the subpoenas, and United States* **Magistrate Judge** *[IDD], the presiding magistrate in the [IDD] case,* **quashed the subpoenas** *in a ruling dated July 28, 1999. Moreover, Magistrate Judge [IDD] indicated that respondent "persists in what can only be described now as a pattern of harassment in an attempt to influence the district judge."*

Thereafter – Thereafter what? The denial of the second recusal motion? The refusal of the Judicial Council to do anything? My clients' confrontation with unwritten court orders requiring them to notify the jailers beforehand, which inmate-witnesses wished to speak with a lawyer – so that prospective witnesses could be singled out and punished? The High Court's selective narrative of "underlying facts" certainly has buried a few uncomfortable ones.

The official storyline ignores all judicial misconduct. My judge lacked the authority to curtail depositions or subpoenas, which were intended to discover the extent of any financial interests he shared with litigators in his court. This evidentiary inquiry ought to have been taken up by the Judicial Council in response to my complaint. The Disciplinary Counsel ought to have completed my judge-aborted inquiry into financial ties between my judge and lawyers with cases in his court. I had asked that this be done. My request was ignored. An attorney who fails to cooperate with the Disciplinary Counsel will face an additional charge of misconduct – but the DC is not required to cooperate with you.

Both the federal judge and the magistrate judge in his employ blocked my inquiry into the judge's financial ties to litigators in his court. The mandatory procedure to be followed was as clear as it was ignored by them. The judge *must* transfer to another court an inquiry into his personal interests in litigation before him. The State Supreme Court knew this, as it was then-controlling authority in the federal courts and had been cited by me in pleadings and also in answers to the Disciplinary Council. The pertinent authority is found at 28 USC 445 (**emphasis** added):

"Any justice, judge, or magistrate of the United States **shall disqualify himself** in any proceeding in which his **impartiality might reasonably be questioned**. (b) He **shall** also **disqualify himself** in the following circumstances: [. . .] He knows that he, individually or as a fiduciary, or his spouse or minor child residing in his household, has **a financial interest in the subject matter in controversy** or in a party to the proceeding, or **any other interest that could be substantially affected by the outcome of the proceeding**; (5) He or his spouse, or a person within the third degree of relationship to either of them, or the spouse of such a person: (i) Is a party to the proceeding, or an officer, director, or trustee of a party; (ii) Is acting as a lawyer in the proceeding; (iii) Is known by the judge to have an interest that could be substantially affected by the outcome of the proceeding."

No lawyer ought to be compelled to argue his clients' matter before a judge whom he believes might be on the take. Bringing his concerns forward, the concerns ought to have been (1) *investigated* by supervising judges and/or (2) *transferred to another judge*, who would make the call about granting access to witnesses and documents. I had asked for both of these remedies. Both were ignored.

Before sanctioning me, the State Supreme Court ought to have cited some authority for the theory that an inquiry into a judge's financial ties to litigators or business entities, is off limits. No such authority exists because that theory is dangerous nonsense. There is no serious, defensible argument, which requires either litigants or litigators to come into court and pretend they have any hope of a fair result, when the judge has been shown to have accepted valuable monetary gifts and done favors to gift-givers, by departing from the procedural rules of his own court.

I had asked the Judicial Council to investigate my judge and to protect me and my clients from him. Documenting his misconduct, I had asked the Judge himself to transfer this case to another court. Discovering prior financial interests between the judge and lawyers who appear before him, I had attempted to discover the extent of these ties – only after the Federal Circuit Judicial Council did nothing about it. My futile attempts to move my clients' matter into another court and to place my complaints about the judge's financial interests before another judge had led to severe penalties levied against me, then to my removal from the lawsuit by the Judge and finally to a public condemnation of me as an unethical lawyer.

In response to the recommendation of the magistrate judge that I be sanctioned by the district judge, I submitted a pleading to the court, stating, in part:

"I will not, without frequent protest, remain in the position of not knowing why a lawsuit was won or lost, whether on the merits of the claims made or because the judge's past conduct has indicated he is willing to accept gratuities. I do not desire to litigate a matter before a court who has (1) accepted a valuable gratuity from litigators with matters mending in the court and (2) explicitly violated a rule of the judicial circuit forbidding publication of the name of a judicial complainant. I have a higher obligation than that to my clients. What shall I tell them? *You would not have lost if you had offered something to the judge?*"

This question remains unanswered. I raise it now, only as a philosophical inquiry. I cannot raise this or ant other issue as an attorney, having been formally deprived of my licenses to practice law, for complaining about the misconduct of a judge.

The decision, once again:

On February 3, 2000, Judge [IDD] **assigned** *the [IDD] case to Magistrate Judge [IDD]* **for pretrial preparation.** *In response, respondent filed a motion to reconsider the assignment to Magistrate Judge [IDD],* **raising the same arguments** *as raised in the two motions to recuse and the two judicial complaints against Judge [IDD].*

Specifically, respondent stated, "the plaintiffs are unwilling to litigate their legal interests before a Court who has received a valuable gratuity from litigators with matters pending in his court. The plaintiffs are also concerned about the Court's fairness, because the Court has improperly published a Judicial Complaint and has identified their counsel as Complainant, thus manifesting an inclination to seek to humiliate and coerce their counsel."

Assigned for pretrial preparation – Since the Judge wanted to keep the matter of his financial ties to litigators away from some other judge, he announced that all this is really about *pretrial preparation*, not fact-based questions directed at his impartiality. So, there is no need to even consider sending this to another judge. *Let's just instruct the Magistrate Judge to get this thing ready for trial!*

Now that the Judicial Council of the Federal Circuit is comfortably on record as having done nothing at all, the Supreme Court can relax a bit. They can proceed in the confidence that the judge's own conclusions about a stubborn ("contumacious") lawyer already have been disposed of by high authority. Yes, I did, yet again, raise the same arguments – because they had been ignored so far. Yet again, they were deemed terrible, sanctionable signs of serious, unethical misconduct. And, yet again, no investigation was conducted. No alarm was sounded. And of course not even a hint of a safe haven was offered to a messenger, bringing unwelcome news about venal judicial misconduct. An attorney, coming forward to protect his clients' lawsuit, can expect just what I received: professional capital punishment.

*Respondent then indicated he may **"seek extra-judicial supervision to enforce the appropriate canons of behavior"** because the [IDD] Circuit was **"unable or unwilling to supervise the district judges as to ethical matters."** Judge [IDD] denied the motion to reconsider on February 28, 2000.*

    seek extra-judicial supervision to enforce the appropriate canons of behavior – Although the State Supreme Court appears to believe that the seeking of extra-judicial supervision is *per se* improper, this is not the case. As the Court knew from submissions I had made, what was contemplated was a possible impeachment or a change in the law. A reference to these approaches ought never become the basis for professional discipline. To do so in the proceedings against me, was an abuse of judicial power. Who will ever come forward to complain of judicial misconduct and, punished, seek a change in the law? I suspect it was to discourage resort to these remedies that I was subjected to public discipline. Incidentally, my letter to the Senate Judiciary Committee, written a decade ago, awaits, still, either an acknowledgement or a response. Turns out, no one wants the $$ spigots turned off.

    What is wrong with telling a court you are considering seeking extra-judicial remedies in light of his misconduct? Is this a threat? Of course it is. But those remedies are certainly lawful. If the State Supreme Court finds fault with even the notion of an impeachment of a judge for accepting gifts and doing favors in return, then the justices ought to be straightforward. They should (1) raise this matter as a count in a complaint, so (2) answer may be given and then the justices might (3) state honestly: we are throwing you out of the legal profession for seeking the impeachment of a federal judge.

the [IDD] Circuit "unable or unwilling to supervise district judges as to ethical matters" – I so stated because supervising judges, who look the other way, are co-conspirators after the fact. For similar misdeeds, judges send malefactors to little rooms with bars at one end and toilets at the other. Since it is impossible to imagine a golden dawn when bribery or conflict-of-interest laws might actually apply to the judiciary, let us at least hope that the stink of unpunished misconduct will lead some of them to resign. They can announce they need to *spend more time with the family* or *let the healing begin*. Or whatever. We do this with other public miscreants, who trade gifts for favors. Judges ought not to be able to give themselves blanket immunity to accept bribes, as they have done.

On April 4, 2000, after Judge [IDD] and Magistrate Judge [IDD] suggested that respondent's conduct may warrant sanctions, **respondent filed a motion seeking a hearing on sanctions**. *In the motion, respondent reurged his request that Judge [IDD] be recused. He also claimed that Judge [IDD] improperly quashed [IDD]'s deposition and reurged his request to depose her. The motion was referred to Magistrate Judge [IDD], who found the following: In this case, it appears that plaintiff's attorney's continued* **attacks** *are calculated to provoke the district judge in an effort toward* **forum shopping**.

52

Cook's attacks appear to be an attempt to influence the result of this case by threats, intimidation and harassment of the district judge. Warnings by the district judge and by the undersigned have not corrected Cook's behavior. Accordingly, **Magistrate Judge** *[IDD]* ordered that respondent be referred to Judge [IDD] for consideration of contempt proceedings, sanctions, and/or referral to the [IDD] Attorney Disciplinary Board. He also **ordered that the clerk of court stop accepting from respondent any pleadings concerning matters raised in the motions to recuse or concerning [IDD]'s deposition.** Finally, he ordered respondent to **learn the [IDD] Rules of Professional Conduct, the Code of Professionalism, and the Code of Professionalism in the Courts adopted by the [IDD] Supreme Court and comply with same** in his activities in and pleadings submitted to the United States District Court, [IDD].*

a hearing on sanctions. Yes. I did ask for a hearing. You are not supposed to be sanctioned without a hearing, after requesting a hearing. But a hearing might have introduced some embarrassing factors into this sorry mix – such as an inquiry into the truth of the matters about which I complained. Of course, I never did get a hearing. Not, as to the recusal motions complaining of the *money-to-me / ruling-for-you* two-step. Not, as to my complaint about the destruction of my ability to represent my clients after being identified as a confidential judicial complainant. Not, as to the refusal of the district judge to forward to another judge my inquiry into his financial dealings with litigators in his court. Not, into the judge's documented part-ownership of a building housing his former law partners. Not, as to the Judge having accepted (as I was told by a lawyer associated with the law firm) annual payments from the judge's former law firm, after becoming a federal judge. Not, into any of the other matters I raised, which sent the supervising judges and the State Supreme Court justices into monkey-see-no-evil mode. Neither the Judge nor the federal Circuit Judicial Council nor the Disciplinary Council nor the State Supreme Court wanted to go anywhere near a hearing that might train the faintest shaft of light upon what the judge had done. Better, far better, to bring this pesky lawyer into a forum where an examination of judicial misconduct is ruled out.

Forum shopping. Yes, I would have liked to have found a judge, who did not accept gifts from parties with an interest in matters coming before the court. Call that dream *forum shopping* if you wish. Too bad one has to shop around for a judge, who does not put his hand in the pockets of litigators.

The Magistrate Judge . . . ordered that the clerk of court stop accepting from respondent any pleadings concerning matters raised in the motions to recuse or concerning [IDD]'s deposition – This order was interpreted to mean that I could not file anything at all, including a motion to stay the Order itself, or to stay subsequent sanctions. My filings were simply returned to me. You are to be gagged before you are shot. With no written record left behind.

On May 31, 2000, Judge [IDD] issued an order **adopting Magistrate Judge [IDD]'s ruling** *and* **ordered respondent to show cause** *why* *he should not be sanctioned. Judge [IDD] sanctioned respondent on June 30, 2000, ordering him to pay $7,500 to the clerk of court and suspending him from practice before the court until he paid the fine. Respondent paid the fine in August 2000.*

Magistrate Judge [IDD]'s ruling – The Magistrate Judge (MJ) was hired by my judge and served at his pleasure. To think for an instant that the Magistrate Judge might have found even a whiff of misconduct on the part of the judge who hired him, who supervised him and who evaluated his job performance . . . this is tooth fairy logic. The rules say *another judge is supposed to hear a complaint about the alleged misconduct of a judge* – not the judge's own employee. The hand-off to the MJ was a sham. This was ridiculous posturing, a pretense, a pantomime, a pretended inquiry, because a legitimate inquiry was neither contemplated nor undertaken. Of all the disappointments encountered in this mess, one of the worst was discovering that a federal Magistrate Judge, sworn to uphold the Constitution, is nothing but a miscreant's stooge.

show cause why he should not be sanctioned – I did show cause why I should not have been sanctioned. I was telling the truth. But the truth was of no concern to anybody in a black robe, since the truth interfered with the pre-determined outcome that required my censure and punishment. The State Supreme Court had no more interest in citing my responses to the show cause orders than my judge or the Magistrate Judge did in reading them. Nothing was going to stop this steamroller. My show cause responses were just more misconduct ammo, evidence of *repeated* references to mere *allegations*.

Between October 25, 2000 and March 6, 2001, respondent was ordered three times to show cause why he should not be sanctioned for **subsequent failures to comply with deadlines and court orders, including orders to cease raising the same issues for which he was previously sanctioned.** *Pursuant to those show cause orders, respondent was ordered to pay $1,243.75 and $1,621.75 in attorney's fees to the defendants on February 22, 2001, fined $2,000 on February 22, 2001, and fined $4,000 on February 26, 2001.*

subsequent failures to comply with deadlines and court orders, including orders to cease raising the same issues for which he was previously sanctioned – Yep. I kept insisting, against all reasonable expectations, that my judge eventually would have to admit that I had been telling the truth. The state Supreme Court declines to specify which deadlines I missed – and for good reason as there were none. The Court also dismissed my responses to show cause orders as mere reiterations of allegations. I finally did just throw in the towel (read on) and admit that my truth-will-prevail gambit was a fantasy in federal court.

Also on February 26, 2001, respondent filed a motion to recuse Magistrate Judge [IDD], citing his April 25, 2000 **order that respondent not interview an inmate** *incarcerated in [IDD], which order respondent claimed was punishment for having filed a judicial complaint against Judge [IDD]. Magistrate Judge [IDD] denied the motion. Respondent paid the attorney's fees, the $2,000 fine, and the $4,000 fine in March 2001.*

Order that respondent not interview an inmate – The State Supreme Court does not cite a doctrine of its own, explaining what is unethical in a lawyer's attempt to interview an inmate without having to give notice to the defendant jailers. For his part, the Magistrate Judge (MJ) was so indifferent to the need of the plaintiffs to interview witnesses without interference from the defendants that he asserted their counsel had violated a "policy" of the state Department of Corrections, by trying to interview a prisoner without prior notice to the jail. There was no such DOC rule. There was merely a notice, typed up at the jail, advising that my clients were required to notify the defendant sheriff before a prisoner/witness might be interviewed. No such *rule* was applied to other attorneys who visited inmates at the prison. My clients were singled out by the jail and the court precisely because of their complaints of serious misconduct by their jailers.

Subjects of interest in my client's lawsuit included: rapes and beatings of prisoners by guards, toilet overflows in this elementary school-turned prison (a building never intended to house anyone), lesbian guards cruising the dormitories (former classrooms) looking for comfort from female prisoners, drug abuse by prisoners and prison guards, the cutting off of inmate phone calls to lawyers. (The defendant sheriff's ownership interest in the phone system was not deemed relevant by my judge. The sheriff's son, I was told, went to the prison from time to time, to clean the prisoners' nickels and quarters out of the pay phones, and walked out with his pockets bulging.)

Neither the defendant jail nor the court itself had the slightest desire for the prisoners to be able to document these matters. *Let's just let the jailers*

*know in advance who wants to talk to the lawyer –
who lives 1,000 miles away – and see if he wants to
make a special trip here. Then, before he can get
here, let's give the talkative prisoner a midnight
transfer to a distant jail; write her up and lock her
down for violating a jail rule that will interfere
with the hoped for parole.*

Had I known that footing the bill for a
judge-junket would grease these particular skids for
my clients, perhaps I could have done what other
lawyers do for their clients. In retrospect this would
have been better for all concerned. The judge gets a
little extra and I could have accomplished so much
more for my clients! I would still be a respected
member of the State Bar – if only I had just slipped
money to a well connected lawyer association, who
could have passed it along to the judge.

I blame Law School. They never offered
Judicial Junkets and the Quid Pro Quo as a
practicum or even as an elective. I blame my clients,
too, those impoverished, imprisoned women. Why
did they have to be poor? Why did they have to get
themselves locked away and abused in a distant jail?

And I blame myself. I should have avoided
impoverished clients, as most lawyers do. Staying
well away from poor litigants is a good idea in a
jurisdiction where a little something extra for the
judge had been past practice. Once on the case, I
should have passed the hat among my clients, even
though some came from homes with a dirt floor. We
would not have come up with enough to send the
judge to Europe but maybe a little gift of
appreciation for his *contribution to the legal
profession* could have done the trick. That sort of
thing has not raised "a shadow of a question" in this
federal circuit. (See footnote, page 97.)

CHAPTER III

OMNIS HOMO MENDAX

At this point in the State Supreme Court Decision, there appears a footnote, which deserves attention. It is footnote 1:

Therefore, because his allegations of misconduct against Judge [IDD] were truthful, respondent argued that he himself did not engage in any misconduct.

Punishing a truth-teller, the Justices adopt an Aristotelian rather than an Augustinian point of view. I am Augustinian. I admit it and admit my error. Augustine wrote, "How can I suitably proceed against lies by lying? Or should robbery be proceeded against by robbery, sacrilege by sacrilege, and adultery by adultery?" This kind of reasoning can get you into trouble. It has gotten me into trouble. It may, again. *Omnis Homo Mendax,* saith Augustine. *All men are liars.* Later on, H.L. Mencken wisely added, "For the habitual truth-teller and truth seeker, the world has very little liking. Run your eye back over the list of martyrs, lay and clerical: nine tenths of them, you will find, stood accused of nothing worse than honest efforts to find out and announce the truth." Where were you, H.L. when I was getting ready to send in my confidential complaint?

The courts have measured Augustine and weighed Aristotle and have gone with the savvy Greek. They know that truth is not a value in and off itself. A truth in court is to be trotted out on a leash, like a mascot. The truth is to be shown around, displayed not for its own sake but to highlight other values. A truth having to do with a judge is acutely subject to the mascot syndrome. This sort of truth must only be displayed under highly controlled circumstances (confidential proceedings), so the real game – the truths and fictions of contestants before them – can be played without undue attention to the *homo mendax* on the bench.

In the courthouse, truth can be taken only in small doses, like morphine. Too much truth and you lose your way. This is pure, 100 proof Aristotle, who wrote, in a book we know as *Ethics*, "To arrive at the truth is indeed the function of intellect in any aspect, but the function of practical intellect is to arrive at the truth that corresponds to right appetition." The judicial appetite regulates the necessary dose of courthouse truth. If you gotta condemn an officer of your own court as unethical, you show some truth, but not all. Why not show it all? You gotta protect the pretention to ethical behavior of the judge. Show maybe a little truth – *the lawyer made allegations about the judge's conduct* – but certainly not a big truth – *the allegations were not investigated because the judicial misconduct actually occurred.*

Aristotle, bless his heart, was worried about the effect of the lie on the deceived. Is withholding some bit of the truth an actual lie? According to Aristotle, only if the deceived become aware of the slight of hand. Aristotle was less worried about the integrity of the deceiver. And here we are back in the courthouse, where the integrity of the judge must be assumed and never questioned.

The "unwritten rule," as it was announced at my disciplinary hearing, is this (I quote from the transcript of the testimony of a Disciplinary Counsel witness, who was cited with approval by the State Supreme Court): "You never mess with a federal judge."

How does it help the standing of the court if this unwritten rule is applied to complaints about judicial misconduct? There is an answer that both subtle Aristotle and principled Augustine would understand. The answer has to do with integrity, or its absence. The Latin root of *integrity* is the same as the root for *untouchable*. An untouchable judge is one who is not touched by a gift from one interested in the outcome of matters before that judge. Avoidance of the gift means the judge's integrity is intact. Unfortunately, in our day, the untouchable judge is one who is immune not from the gift but from the touch of any truthful accusation of gift-giving. For the person of principle, being untouched by an accusation of accepting the gift is not the same as being untouched by the gift. But the shabbier rule is good enough around the federal courthouse, where you are treated to the spectacle of a judge with his hand out and the power to make everyone look the other way.

I swung, though not soon enough, over to pragmatic Aristotle and away from saintly Augustine. My delay was caused because I had not yet read Mencken or that footnote in my state Supreme Court decree, about the truth being a mere chimera around the courthouse. But I did, finally, get it. I realized that when it comes to judges, a show of integrity is just as good as actual integrity, better in fact, since the judge gets to keep the money and the gifts and take the trips (first class?) with the costs footed by people who are interested in the judge's judicial function.

On March 26, 2001, he filed a pleading in which **he apologized to the court**, *explaining that he recognizes his* **conduct went "beyond the permissible limits of advocacy.**" *Respondent also filed, under seal, a motion to withdraw as counsel of record for the [IDD] plaintiffs. Respondent was dismissed as counsel on May 10, 2001.*

Before I apologized, my judge ordered me to do so. He also ordered me to withdraw from the lawsuit if I were to avoid additional sanctions. The State Supreme Court might have admitted this as a fact. But to note the Judge's threat of further sanctions as the trigger for an apology would have introduced an unsavory element of coercion into the apology. The Justices did not want to acknowledge coercion of an officer of their court. The pretense of judicial integrity required that coercion of the complainant be mischaracterized as the purest exercise of free will. The lawyer-defendant must be seen as admitting to wrongdoing for his errant *allegations*. A show trial requires a confession. A coerced confession is better than no confession at all, if that is what your Aristotelian appetites dictate.

beyond the permissible limits of advocacy – It is true, or was in my case: a complaint to supervising judges that the judge of your impoverished clients' case not have business ties to parties with their own interest in judicial outcomes controlled by the judge – this is advocacy beyond permissible limits.

When it comes to complaints of judicial misconduct, the dangerous depths begin at the water's edge. You can reach into the slime if you must, but no one wants to look upon the writhing, smelly, slippery object you happen to grasp. Better to throw that bottom-feeder back into the muck and pretend you were never there. Just walk away. If you do not walk away, a standard somewhere south of the truth will be imposed upon you anyway, by supervising judges. The solons will wisely, gently prod you back upon the sunlit path to lawyerly income, where you will bask in the glow of your peers' respect – members with you, in what is called, for some reason, a "profession."

Do not believe for an instant that an attorney is obligated to come forward if evidence exists that a judge has committed a violation of the rules of judicial conduct, which raise a question about the judge's fitness to continue as a judge. You must never mind what Rule 8.3. of the Rules of Professional Conduct (Reporting Professional Misconduct), suggests (emphasis **added**):

(b) *A lawyer having knowledge that a judge has committed a violation of applicable rules of judicial conduct that raises a substantial question as to the judge's fitness for office **shall** inform the appropriate authority.*

These words on the page are merely words on a page. My ordeal makes it quite clear: forget about it. Look with Aristotle to the *appetition* of the judge and of the supervising judges and you will see your miscalculation. Remember the unwritten rule

– *never mess with a judge* – and take it to heart. The spigot is wide open. Perhaps it was different, some while ago. Justice Benjamin Cardozo returned gifts from lawyers, saying, gently, "It was a graceful and friendly thing for you to do. But . . . I am going to send it back to you. I am fussy about receiving gifts." Cardozo was an Augustinian, not an Aristotelian but he has been dead for decades.

Justice Cardozo said something else, which ought to be pertinent to judicial misconduct, but is not. Cardozo stated that a "fundamental and unquestioned" principle is that "no one shall be permitted to . . . take advantage of his own wrong." *R.H. Stearns Co. v. United States*, 291 U.S. 54 (pp.61-62). I took this to mean that if a judge has accepted a gift and favored the gift giver, he may not compound his misconduct by using his judicial authority to block inquiries into financial interests he shares with litigators or into other aspects of his own misconduct. This argument, and each of my other arguments, was disposed of by simply ignoring it. Proceeding in this manner, the State Supreme Court can easily move from its selection of the damning "salient facts" to my

DISCIPLINARY PROCEEDINGS

Formal Charges

On April 28, 2004, the ODC filed one count of formal charges against respondent, alleging that his conduct violated Rules 3.1 (meritorious claims and contentions), 4.4 (respect for the rights of third persons), 8.4(a) (violation of the Rules of Professional Conduct), and 8.4(d) (engaging in conduct prejudicial to the administration of justice) of the Rules of Professional Conduct. **Respondent answered the formal charges, essentially denying the allegations of misconduct.**

denying the allegations of misconduct – There is that word *allegations* again. To be clear, I denied the *characterization* of what I did as misconduct. I did what they said I did. I asked the judge to recuse himself. I filed a confidential complaint with the Judicial Council of the federal Circuit. I responded to show cause orders and filed motions for reconsideration – and in all of these, I re-urged the remedies I was seeking and re-stated the factual basis for these pleadings.

No one who has condemned me for *alleged* lawyerly misconduct has ever suggested that anything I *alleged* about judicial misconduct was not true. It is all a question of characterization. You are *found* guilty. You are *found* innocent. But if the issue is not you but your conduct, then a finding of misconduct ought to be announced only after the *allegations* have been proven up or down. It is not my integrity but the *alleged* integrity of the disciplinary process that may be questioned, since not the slightest effort was expended in running down any of my *allegations*. My own efforts to get to the factual bottom of the judge's misconduct was taken as improper, additional evidence of my own misbehavior.

Like a Model T driven by Stan Laurel, the disciplinary proceedings ran in reverse; they worked backward from the urgency to discover something wrong with a lawyer, so as to protect the chimeral prestige of a judge. Missing was even the honest acknowledgement that the initial charges against me simply melted away and new and different misconduct was *alleged* - without my having an opportunity to defend myself. In these disciplinary proceedings, I was charged with complaining about a judge but convicted of failing to file an appeal. There was no need to withdraw one absurd charge when a new, equally absurd one has been substituted for it. (See page 146.) I was placed in a procedure which ruled out my fundamental defense – my own truthful complaints about the judge's obvious misconduct. In this parody, any awkward facts were simply ignored. Procedural integrity, like my own truthful statements were both subordinated to another interest: the need to find something wrong with the lawyer's behavior, so that the judge's conduct is never at issue.

Formal Hearing

This matter proceeded to a formal hearing on the merits. Respondent participated in the hearing via telephone. The ODC called [IDD] (defense counsel in the [IDD] case), **Magistrate Judge** *[IDD], and [IDD]* (**defense counsel** *in the [IDD] case) to testify before the committee. Respondent did not testify on his own behalf, nor did the ODC call him to testify.*

(Footnote 2: **[IDD]** *testified that respondent engaged in "**almost constant warfare with the judge**" during the case. Respondent also filed* **redundant pleadings**, *raising the same issues over and over again, which had to be responded to and ruled on each time,* **making the case go on longer than normal.** *Since she billed by the hour, respondent's redundant pleadings caused her to bill her clients two to three times more in*

*attorney's fees than **normal**. While she felt that respondent had the **"best of intentions,"** she also felt he **"stepped over the line,"** was **"misguided,"** and **"got carried away about the judge."**)*

*(Footnote 3: [IDD] testified that respondent filed redundant pleadings and began to focus more on Judge [IDD], making **"outlandish" accusations** against the judge, which diverted time and attention away from the merits of the case. [IDD] also testified that he had to bill his clients for the time he spent on the redundant issues. Finally, he testified that the case was **concluded approximately six months after respondent was dismissed**.)*

The only witnesses adverse to me at the hearing was the Magistrate Judge (employed by the judge) and two opposing counsel. The lawyer-witnesses testified that I had engaged in the following sorts of misdeeds:

almost constant warfare with the judge - redundant pleadings - making the case go on longer than normal - bill more attorney's fees than normal - respondent had the "best of intentions" but "stepped over the line," was "misguided," and "got carried away about the judge"

More questions now arise, to be added to the myriad unanswered questions which this parody has already occasioned. (See pages 41, 49.) Is there no obligation (by the Court or the Hearing Committee) to identify my so-called "redundant" pleadings and to demonstrate their redundancy? to compare the duration of this jail case and its 100-plus plaintiffs with a so-called "routine" jail case? to acknowledge that the livelihood of each of the adverse witnesses was at risk (as mine already was) - if they found fault with the behavior of a federal district judge?

I am heartened to know that a witness against me concluded that I had "the best of intentions." But let's get behind this patronizing throw-away line. What were those intentions? To keep my clients from losing their lawsuit because their lawyer had failed to gift the judge? To protect myself from financial ruin and professional destruction after the Federal Circuit Judicial Council failed to investigate my fact-laden complaints about the district judge? To try to salvage a lawsuit after the judge, in violation of the rules of the Judicial Council, publicly identified me as a confidential complainant? What part of my conduct had been *misguided*? Had I been misguided by the Federal Circuit Rules, which state that my identity would be protected if I made a confidential complaint to the supervising judges? Had I been misguided by the Rules of Professional Conduct, which mandate that a lawyer "shall" report judicial misconduct? Had I been misguided by the high-sounding phrases in these Rules, suggesting that an officer of the court must zealously represent his clients? or by rhetoric which implies protection for a lawyer who is mandated to come forward and report the misconduct of a judge?

Both respondent and the ODC introduced **documentary evidence** *at the hearing.*

I did submit *documentary evidence,* quite a bit of it; and virtually all of the documents I submitted were never noticed, commented upon or cited at all. These items included copies of filings with the state's Secretary of State, which showed that the district judge was an owner of the building which housed his former law firm. There were documents (pleadings from the lawsuit), which identified persons who had stated to me that the judge may have received payments from his old law firm, after he became a federal judge. Apparently, by coming forward to document this arrangement, an officer of the court may be characterized as having gotten *carried away about the judge* and must be drummed out of the legal profession.

I documented that the federal Circuit Judicial Council had declined to produce any information in the disciplinary proceedings that the Council had in its possession. But the hearing committee was as uninterested in such matters as the prosecutor had been and as the State Supreme Court would prove to be. I also submitted my own exhibits (fifty, in all), some of which indicated how pointless it would have been to appeal the District Judge's shenanigans to the Federal Circuit, since the judges on the Circuit not only accept gifts arranged for them by litigators and litigants but they are inclined to belittle – publicly (see note, page 97) – anyone who might object to this. I also documented my request to the Disciplinary Counsel to refer this matter to a United States Attorney. Nothing happened. All of my documents disappeared into the Black Hole of what should have been an even-handed disciplinary process. It never was any such thing, nor was it intended to be such.

From the perspective of the supervising judges the money spigot has got to remain open at all hazards. Anyway, the only person running a hazard is someone who thinks judges must not accept gifts from parties with an interest in the outcome of matters before the court.

Hearing Committee Recommendation

*After considering this matter, the hearing committee made **factual findings** as follows:*

*The **first sign of trouble** in the [IDD] case appeared on June 26, 1998 when respondent filed a pleading in which he moved the court to "investigate its own docket and determine whether this Court has ever permitted representative civil rights plaintiffs to proceed as class representatives." In the same pleading, respondent **implied** that Judge [IDD] had engaged in efforts to dissuade an attorney from enrolling as co-counsel for the plaintiffs. Respondent made similar **insinuations** in his response to a court order dated December 30, 1998.*

a *sign of trouble* – is NOT a factual finding anymore than are the characterizations of my statements as *implied* or as *insinuations*. The hearing committee, like the Court itself, is merely working backward, from a conclusion of misconduct, fishing around for a way to justify this conclusion. (For further discussion of this *sign of trouble*, see page 10-13.)

implied . . . insulations - If the committee, and the court, were actually concerned for the truth of matters associated with this proceeding, they would not have labeled my statements *insinuations*, without stating, clearly, what made them so and what factors kept them from being literal facts.

*Respondent then filed a motion to recuse Judge [IDD], accusing him of partiality in favor of a litigant's attorney who was a member of Judge [IDD]'s former law firm and, as president of a legal association, arranged for Judge [IDD] to travel to Italy **to address the association's meeting**. The motion was denied, and in reasons for denying the motion, Judge [IDD] **referred** to the fact that respondent filed a judicial complaint against him. Respondent then filed another motion to recuse, alleging that Judge [IDD] violated Rule 15 of the [IDD] Circuit's Rules Governing Complaints of Judicial Misconduct or Disability, which **mandates that judicial complaints remain confidential**.*

    to address the association's meeting – The judge's overseas trip was comped by a lawyers' association, some of whose members had interests in matters in his court. To my amazement, two members of the group I had complained about had been assigned to the 3-person committee that decided I should lose my law license. Why didn't these lawyers step aside, in a matter having to do with a formal complaint about their association gifting a judge? None of the players in the *money-to-me ruling-for-you* parody can opt out later on. If someone actually admits to a conflict of interest, the entire shabby arrangement will come to light.

    referred to the fact that respondent filed a judicial complaint against him – Referred? This is a seriously incomplete and thus a false statement. As I mentioned earlier (page 42) the Judge did not merely *refer* to something or other. He *attached to a ruling the decision of the Judicial Counsel*, and then ordered me to pay $7500 into the court.

71

Federal *Circuit's Rules Governing Complaints of Judicial Misconduct or Disability, which mandates that judicial complaints remain confidential* – At last, we are getting somewhere. At last, there is an acknowledgement that the federal judicial complaint rules require a complaint about a judge's misconduct be treated with confidentiality. As I read this decision for the first time, I relaxed a bit. Now, there surely must follow a finding that my Judge did in fact violate the rules. And if he violated the rules, then, of course, I cannot be made out to be an unethical lawyer for having filed a motion of recusal or for having formally complained about this misconduct. No such luck. The subject was quickly changed.

Judge [IDD]'s relationship with the aforementioned attorney became a topic of **intense scrutiny** *for respondent. On June 29, 1999, [IDD] objected to respondent's subpoena for the following records:* **checks made payable to Judge [IDD] from 1984 to the present; checks made payable to Judge [IDD]'s wife from 1984 to present; and checks made payable to any party, which might benefit Judge [IDD], his wife, or any of his relatives.** *[IDD] objected to an identical subpoena. On July 28, 1999,* **Magistrate Judge [IDD] ruled** *that the requested records in the subpoenas were irrelevant and the subpoenas themselves were harassing.*

intense scrutiny – I am criticized and ultimately drummed out of the legal profession for giving not scrutiny but "intense" scrutiny. Would *casual* scrutiny have been OK? The high court's hyperbole betrays a desire to find something wrong with me, and also to send a message to the legal community: we are not going to let you scrutinize documents that might prove judicial misconduct.

checks made payable to Judge [IDD] from 1984 to the present; checks made payable to Judge [IDD]'s wife from 1984 to present; and checks made payable to any party, which might benefit Judge [IDD], his wife, or any of his relatives – Yes. I would like to have had access to these documents. Yes. They were relevant to my complaints that the judge had been in a financial relation with litigators in his court. No. neither the Judicial Council nor the Disciplinary Counsel, nor the disciplinary hearing committee nor the State Supreme Court displayed the slightest interest in getting to the bottom of this. There is no reason to get to the bottom of an allegation of financial ties between a judge and litigators, when the easiest and safest route is simply to take away the law license of the attorney who complains about this sort of thing.

The *Magistrate Judge . . . ruled* – As I mentioned earlier (page 55) the magistrate judge was an employee of this federal district judge who blocked the inquiry. When a question arises concerning the personal interest of a judge, the rules state that the matter is to be referred to another judge – certainly not to an employee of the very judge who is the subject of the investigation. The Judicial Counsel knew of this slight of hand by the judge, and ignored it. So did the Disciplinary Counsel, as did the hearing committee in its turn and also the Disciplinary Board. And of course, so did the State Supreme Court – assuming the Justices read the record of the case – as they announced in their Decision that they had. (See pp. 9-10 above.)

Why did all of these guardians of the ethics of the legal profession overlook the judge's deliberate circumvention of the prescribed procedure? My theory is that we are dealing once again with the open spigot syndrome. If you allow an investigation into *one* judge for having a financial relationship with litigators, where will it end? It might not end and then, the spigot might get shut off. The be-robed ethicists have placed themselves in charge of deciding just how much money to themselves is too much and how many gifts are too many. They are not anxious to shut off the $$ spigot, which may in fact be a high pressure hose.

On July 13, 1999, respondent filed a request that the above objections be **transferred to another court for consideration**.

transferred to another court for consideration – I am surprised to find this reference to my motion, in which I asked that the proper procedures be followed. No matter. The Justices recover themselves and do not mention that this motion is denied. A reader of the Decision is left with the impression that my asking for *another judge to rule* on a federal judge's financial ties to litigators is merely one more example of my misconduct. The Judges know better. And we know they know better because *Omnis Homo Mendax*.

SOURCES

Aristotle, on integrity, see *The Ethics of Aristotle, The Nichomechean Ethics*, (1976: Penguin Books, page 205)

H.L. Mencken, on the risks of telling the truth: "Pater Patriae," *The Vintage Mencken* (1990: Vintage Books, Alistair Cooke, editor, page 72)

Saint Augustine, on lying, quoted in Sissela Bok, *Lying, Moral Choice in Public and Private Life* (1979: Random House, Vintage, page 267)

I am going to send it back to you. I am fussy about receiving gifts – Benjamin Cardozo returns a gift from a lawyer. Cited in *Cardozo*, by Andrew L. Kaufman (Harvard University Press 1998, page 186)

MAL CAMINO MAL DESTINO

No longer permitted to practice law, I wait to one side. My crimes: demands to a miscreant judge to step aside; confidential complaints to supervising judges; an aborted inquiry into the miscreant's ties to lawyers with court business - blocked by the miscreant. My many convictions: interference with the administration of "justice" by the miscreant; burdening lawyer-witnesses, whom guardians of judicial privilege decline to examine.

Questions which stop the ears of the guardians: How many judges receive money gifts from parties with court business? How many do favors in return? How many such judges are too many? One hundred? Ten? One? Not so few as one. Better to blacken the reputation of an officer of the court than to admit to one.

An information asymmetry: the robed miscreant accepts the gift(s) and does the judicial favor(s). The imprudent court officer denounces the miscreant. One is *distinguished*; one is tossed out of the miscreant *profession*. What is professed, thereby?

When the conduct of a robed miscreant is placed in issue, plenary investigative tools (under the control of judges) become as flaccid and useless as a third nipple. You states, whose judges punish lawyers for not gifting them. Your Counsels of Discipline blend the power of lions with the prestige of dung beetles. What are they afraid of? Judicial spite? What do they know that we cannot know? That gifts and favors to/from a robed miscreant are routine?

No Gifts Accepted - All Gifts Returned. This was the Cardozo Rule. The road from Benjamin Cardozo to this moment has been a long, downward strut and shuffle.

I have nothing but respect for the judges. Nothing. That's the problem.

RBC, *That's What I'm Talking About,* page 51

CHAPTER IV

- DODJI -
DOCTRINE OF
DELIBERATE JUDICIAL
IGNORANCE

On July 16, 1999, respondent deposed [IDD], questioning her about the same matters that were the subjects of the above subpoenas. However, [IDD]'s attorney objected to the taking of the deposition and instructed her not to answer. Thus, during the deposition, the parties called Judge [IDD] to resolve the issue, and **Judge [IDD] disallowed any questioning of [IDD]**.

Judge . . . disallowed any questioning – The Canons of Judicial Ethics specify that a judge is not to rule on matters which touch his business or financial interests. When I raised this issue directly with my judge, he ignored me. It was as if I had never spoken. In law school you do not learn about DODJI - the DOCTRINE OF DELIBERATE JUDICIAL IGNORANCE. If a court finds an inquiry or an argument unpleasant or embarrassing, it is free (apparently) to ignore it. My removal from the attorney rolls could serve as a study in the workings of DODJI.

In response to Judge [IDD]'s February 3, 2000 order assigning the [IDD] case to Magistrate Judge [IDD] for **pretrial preparation**, respondent filed a request to refer the case to another district court *because the plaintiffs did not want to litigate their issues before a judge who "received a valuable gratuity from litigators with matters pending in his court" and who "improperly published a Judicial Complaint and has identified their counsel as a Complainant, thus manifesting an inclination to seek to humiliate and coerce their counsel."*

pretrial preparation – The judge had had enough of me and of this case. He had no intention of permitting my complaints about him to be investigated or resolved in a transparent, objective fashion. After dodging my motions accusing him of conflicts of interests, it was now time to destroy the case. This is what was done. Instead of dealing with the myriad issues which brought his own ethical conduct into question, the judge characterized the case as - ready for trial! In this way, my further complaints about his misconduct could be subsequently interpreted as delaying tactics. Of course, the Magistrate Judge (MJ) went along with this. As an employee supervised by the judge, what else could he do? Well, what he could have done was to blow the whistle himself on these maneuvers and make independent rulings, as one might hope would be the case in any tribunal before any adjudicator in the federal system. The slavish, sycophantic posturing of magistrate judges is one more, sad secret in our federal court system. These individuals are there to work the will of the life-appointed, powerful judicial officer who has hired them. MJ duties include protecting the judge from truthful, factual complaints of misconduct; their duties do not encompass making decisions that might embarrass the judge.

In response to respondent's motions to recuse Judge [IDD], **Magistrate Judge** *[IDD] suggested that their* **frivolous nature might lead to sanctions.**

frivolous nature might lead to sanctions – In principle, a frivolous recusal motion could very well lead to sanctions. But "frivolous," in these proceedings, was not an assessment based on any degree of analysis. It is a characterization, a conclusion. Where is the investigation? Where is it shown that the judge had NOT accepted a trip to Europe by parties interested in his judicial function? Where is it documented that he had NOT bent the rules of his own court so as to reward his former law firm? Where may one find the statement that the judge did NOT violate the judicial complaint rules by identifying me as a confidential complainant? Where is it written that no rules violation occurred when my judge attached the Judicial Council decision to an order of his own? Where do we find the statement from the magistrate judge that the district judge had NOT ruled on matters having to do with his personal financial interests?

One looks in vain for simple honesty from the Justices. My judge actually did engage in all of these shenanigans. But in order to find misconduct in me six and seven years after the events themselves, a State Supreme Court decided it would be better to parrot the earlier, flawed proceedings and conclude that all of my complaints were "frivolous."

The court did not order sanctions *or order respondent to show cause why he should not be sanctioned. However,* **on his own motion, respondent sought a hearing on sanctions,**

79

taking this opportunity to also reiterate his allegations of misconduct against Judge [IDD] and his request to depose [IDD]. *In response, Magistrate Judge [IDD] listed twenty-eight incidents of respondent's behavior he felt warranted sanctions.* Respondent **reacted** to this ruling by **reiterating his previous allegations** against Judge [IDD].

on his own motion, respondent sought a hearing on sanctions – Jurisprudence in the federal courts used to disfavor a delay between a threat to impose sanctions and any subsequent punishment. Sanctions had been threatened against me and I did not want this hanging over my head, while I attempted to represent my clients, file additional motions, etc, before a judge, who had raised the specter of sanctions but not yet imposed them. I also knew by now that the supervising judges of the Federal Circuit were not going to investigate this court, so I asked for a hearing on the issue of sanctions.

The court did not order sanctions - The Justices took no notice of jurisprudence, which requires a prompt resolution, once a judge has threatened to impose sanctions. In light of the threat, I moved for a hearing. Lacking candor, the Justices fail to note that no hearing was ever permitted. Such a hearing would have examined not only the basis or reasonableness of any sanctions – since I was telling the truth. Such a hearing might have produced additional evidence of misconduct. This is the reason (I believe) why a hearing was never permitted.

taking this opportunity to also reiterate his allegations – This is a reference to arguments made in my motion for a hearing. When you bring a motion, you are supposed to present an argument as to why the motion ought to be granted. But it better suited the Justices not to take note of the need to submit an *argument in support*. Instead, they preferred to take the arguments appended to my motion for sanctions and characterize them as some kind of improper reiteration of "allegations."

I suppose it ought to be said, yet again, that the only way to confer upon *allegations* either the dignity of truth or the ignominy of falsehood is to investigate them. The question that hangs over this judicial travesty is this: why was an investigation never conducted? An inquiry was avoided at every turn, first by the subject federal judge, then by his employee, the Magistrate Judge, then by the Chief Judge of the Federal Circuit, then by the Judicial Council of the Circuit, then by the Disciplinary Counsel and finally by the State Supreme Court. Someday, somehow, a bright light must be trained on the dark corners of the courthouse, where gifts are offered and accepted, and the judicial function is conformed to the needs of the pay-as-you-go hustlers for judicial favors, and where professional punishment is administered to the honest but friendless critic of this sordid behavior.

In response – Instead of granting the motion requesting a hearing, the district judge referred the matter to the MJ, his employee, with a mandate to work up a list of misdeeds, which could then be taken as evidence of my misconduct. By way of this maneuver, the judge was excusing himself from ever having to admit or deny any of the factual statements I had made, which documented his misconduct.

Magistrate Judge [IDD] listed twenty-eight incidents of respondent's behavior he felt warranted sanctions. Actually, the Magistrate Judge listed twenty-nine. It needs to be stressed that this recommendation of sanctions was made by the judge's own assistant, a United States Magistrate Judge (See pages 55, 73).

In 2000, in compliance with my obligation as an officer of the court to report any sanctions, I myself forwarded the MJ's findings to the State Supreme Court – together with my responses (see page 116-34, below). This communication was never acknowledged by the Court – until the Disciplinary Counsel opened its investigation of me, two years later (see page 144, below). Here are the 29 incidents, which are cited as warranting sanctions (**emphasis** added) – with my comments:

Cook is hereby notified that sanctions may be considered based on the following:

1. *Persisting in re-arguing issues after they have been denied by the court and **after the time for asking for reconsideration has expired, Fed.R.Civ.P. 59(b)**, specifically (a) **allegations** relative to the issues raised in the first motion to recuse [Doc 383, 388, 389] the **desire to depose** [IDD] [Doc 388, 399] and (c) **allegations** relative to the second motion to recuse [Doc 388, 389]. The court notes that no motion for reconsideration was filed by plaintiffs' attorney with regard to any of these matters.)*

after the time for asking for reconsideration has expired, Fed.R.Civ.P. 59(b) – This rule has no

82

relevance to a motion for sanctions; the rule reads: "(b) Time to File a Motion for a New Trial. A motion for a new trial must be filed no later than 10 days after the entry of judgment."

Allegations – Yet again, truthful statements about judicial misconduct are neutered by calling them mere *allegations.*

the desire to depose – Oh desire of my heart! How much more comfortable for the subject judge – how dismissive – to characterize an effort to actually investigate a matter as a wistful desire, instead of a strategy, a decision, a consequence, a duty – or an embarrassment to the supervising judges of the Federal Circuit, who will not take up the unpalatable task of getting to the bottom of factual assertions of misconduct by a district judge. After the supervising judges avoid their duty of supervision, the task of getting to the bottom of the muck in the courthouse is left to the friendless officer of their court.

2. ***Persisting*** *in complaints concerning the district judge, which complaints were raised in the first motion to recuse [Doc 315] after the motion to recuse was denied [Doc 322, 330] and after receipt of a copy of the [IDD]* ***Circuit decision*** *(attached to Document 330)* ***rejecting plaintiff's attorney's claims.***

Persisting in complaints concerning the district judge – Yes. I confess. I did persist, and learned a terrible lesson. If an officer of the court persists, even confidentially, in trying to get an honest and straightforward response to complaints of judicial misconduct, the career of that lawyer will be brought to an expensive, public and humiliating end.

83

[Federal] *Circuit* *decision* *(attached* *to* *Document* *330)* *rejecting* *plaintiff's* *attorney's* *claims* – We live in an era of self-congratulation as to our know-how and our know-what. But, even from this high perch, I confess: there has not yet been invented a machine that can measure the deceiving cynicism of this statement by the Magistrate Judge. The referenced decision is a confidential one from the Judicial Council – not a published decision of a federal circuit court. This is a fact the Magistrate Judge finds advantageous to overlook, and does so repeatedly in his recitation of my alleged misconduct.

By declining to mention that the decision comes from the Judicial Council, the MJ is not thus confronted with an embarrassment: by rule, this decision was based on a *confidential* complaint, and was drafted in the confidential chambers of the Federal Circuit Judicial Council, and not intended to be published. By further rule it could not be made public except by leave of the chief judge of the Circuit. In deliberate misstatement of these facts, the MJ may then use the appearance of the Judicial Council decision against the complainant, whose truthful complaint about the judge thus becomes, by way of this distortion, a helpful fantasy, vague but telling evidence of not judge but lawyer misconduct.

rejecting plaintiff's attorney's claims – The theoretically confidential complaint was *rejected* by judges, who themselves enjoy gifts from litigators and others with an interest in outcomes determined by the judges themselves (see footnote, page 97). These judges look the other way when their confidential decision is trotted out publicly, at the personal convenience of the judge who was the subject of the complaint. These same judges did not question the truthfulness of the complaint(s). They could not. The district judge did what I said he did. The issue is: can he get away with it? The answer, supplied by his supervisors: Yes, indeed.

3. *Filing two motions to recuse (Doc 315 339)* **without making reasonable inquiry into the facts** *upon which they were based.*

without making reasonable inquiry into the facts – The two recusal motions are part of the record. Without reproducing these pleadings, which are public documents and thus open to examination by anyone, perhaps the best way to respond to the notion that a reasonable inquiry into the facts was not made, would be to reproduce my written response to the formal charges of misconduct, which were filed against me in 2004. Here are excerpts from that response, with names deleted and without any of the some fifty exhibits attached.

Judge [IDD] Engaged in Misconduct.

The undersigned acknowledges that he brought motions of recusal before United States District Court Judge [IDD]. The undersigned further acknowledges that he filed two confidential complaints against Judge [IDD] with the Chief Judge and with the Judicial Counsel of the [IDD] Federal Circuit. (Please see appended Exhibits 4 through 10)[1] In response to the

---

[1] There is additional correspondence between the undersigned and the [IDD] Circuit (clerk) concerning these two complaints. This material is

second Complaint, the Chief Judge of the [IDD] Circuit declined to accept the invitation of the respondent either to order the recusal of Judge [IDD] or to investigate further the Complaint. However, <u>the Chief Judge found that Judge [IDD] had in fact violated the Judicial Complaint rules by publishing the name of the undersigned as a Judicial Complainant</u>. (Appended Exhibit 9.)[2] In an ongoing serious absence of candor before this Board, the Disciplinary Counsel seeks to sanction the Respondent - without informing this Board that Judge [IDD] engaged in the complained of misconduct.

The gist of the recusal motions and of the Judicial Counsel complaints, were that Judge [IDD] engaged in misconduct, as follows:

---

not appended but promptly will be forwarded to this Board if requested. The undersigned suggested to the Disciplinary Counsel that all of this material be reviewed prior to the filing of Formal Charges.

[2] Judge [IDD], for the Judicial Counsel, stated that this rule violation does not constitute "conduct prejudicial to the effective and expeditious administration of the business of the courts." This finding suggests there are two sets of rules: one for Judicial Complainants and another for the judges and that if in fact an officer of the court brings a <u>truthful</u> complaint before the Judicial Counsel, one can only expect to be exposed to punishment by the very judge who is the subject of the complaint.

1. that Judge [IDD] accepted a significant gift from an organization whose president was a former law partner of the judge and was, **at the time the gift was made, simultaneously litigating a matter before Judge [IDD]** (Appended Exhibits 11 and 12);

2. that **Judge [IDD] violated the Local Rules of his court as well as the Federal Rules of Civil Procedure** (as interpreted by the U.S. Supreme Court) by granting a motion to amend a complaint without permitting the adverse party to respond or to participate in a hearing on the merits;

3. that **Judge [IDD]**, contrary to the federal judicial complaint rules, **published the name of the Respondent as a confidential complainant to the Judicial Council**.

4. that Judge [IDD] improperly issued orders quashing a deposition related to the inquiry into possible improper financial dealings between Judge [IDD] and attorneys with business in his court.[3]

---

[3] This aborted discovery was an attempt by the undersigned to protect himself and his clients from a misbehaving federal district judge. Since the Judicial Counsel declined to investigate Judge [IDD], the undersigned sought to do so, seeking

Judge [IDD] did in fact engage in all of these acts of misconduct. The undersigned also submitted documents to the Judicial Counsel, which showed:

5. That **Judge** [IDD] was in a real estate partnership through which he **was the landlord of his former law firm - while serving as a United States District Judge**. (Exhibit 16)

A complaint was lodged with the Judicial Counsel about this arrangement. The Judicial Counsel was also asked by the undersigned to investigate this arrangement. The complaint was denied and the Judicial Counsel declined to conduct an investigation.

The undersigned also asked the Disciplinary Counsel to investigate this matter, prior to the filing of formal charges. An investigation by the Disciplinary Counsel would be proper because (1) the Disciplinary Counsel has a duty to investigate charges of attorney misconduct, (2) the other partners with the Judge are lawyers and (3) because fundamental fairness requires that the Disciplinary Counsel ascertain the truth prior to the filing of Formal Charges. The request by the undersigned to the Disciplinary Counsel to investigate the real

---

sworn testimony from a former managing partner of the [IDD] Law Firm.

estate partnership has not been acknowledged.

Because the authorities empowered to investigate the allegations made have apparently not done so, the Respondent is left with no means to confirm the details of Judge [IDD]'s business ties with lawyers appearing in his court - prior to the adjudication of this matter by this Board. (Please see the discussion, *supra*, at footnote 4.) This procedural unfairness serves to insulate a United States District Judge from a legitimate ethical inquiry into the court's allegedly improper ties to lawyers appearing before the court.

Details of the misconduct of Judge [IDD], which prompted recusal motions, other properly submitted pleadings and confidential formal Judicial Counsel complaints here follow.

1. The $4,500 Travel Gift

Judge [IDD]'s former law partner (1) was President of the [IDD] (2) sat on the [IDD] committee that decided who would be offered a gift of travel to [IDD] and (3) was simultaneously litigating a case before Judge [IDD] when the gift was made. (Exhibits 11 & 12). This gift-giving gave an appearance of impropriety and was, therefore, an appropriate basis of complaint against Judge [IDD].

2. Judge [IDD] violated the Local Rules of his own Court and the Federal Rules of Civil

<u>Procedure to the benefit of a former law partner.</u>

On November 17, 1997, a motion to amend a complaint in [IDD] was filed before Judge [IDD], over the objection of adverse parties. On November 18, 1997 - *the next day* - Judge [IDD] granted this motion. Local Rule [IDD] of the Local Rules of Court requires that, objection to the filing of an amended complaint having been made, a hearing on the matter must be set. Judge [IDD] simply ignored this rule of his own court. Furthermore, Rule 15(a) of the Federal Rules of Procedure, while permitting a court to grant leave to amend a complaint, has been interpreted by the Supreme Court to require a district court to consider "bad faith" [. . .] "dilatory motive" [. . .] "prejudice to the opposing party" before granted leave to amend a complaint. <u>Foman v. Davis</u>, 371 U.S. 178, 182 (1962).

The attorney who brought the motion to amend the Complaint was a former law partner of the Judge. (Exhibit 13) Following the amendment, the case settled for $1.7 million. The local press reported (Exhibit 14) that one of the counsel in [IDD] believed that "most" of the $1.1 million portion of the settlement paid by an insurance company would go to the plaintiff's lawyers. These shenanigans by Judge [IDD] - permitting a complaint to be amended in violation of the Local Rules as well as the Federal Rules of Civil Procedure - apparently netted hundreds of thousands of dollars for his former law firm; this conduct was an appropriate basis of complaint against Judge [IDD]. Therefore, the bringing of such a complaint by the undersigned does not violate the Rules of Professional Conduct.

[. . .] In [IDD], the clients of the undersigned were poor, incarcerated, predominantly Black women, locked up in [IDD], doing state time in a school house converted into a prison. Their lawsuit against the [IDD] and Sheriff [IDD] had to do with repeated physical and sexual abuse by their guards and also included detailed allegations of reprisal and physical abuse if they attempted to communicate with an attorney about their mistreatment. These women were in no position to offer Judge [IDD] a trip to Europe in order to influence the outcome of their lawsuit - or to ask their counsel to engineer a gift through some attorney organization in which he might have influence.

[. . .] Judicial Counsel rulings do not protect an officer of the federal courts, who files a confidential judicial complaint in good faith. On the contrary, these rulings (from which there is no appeal) protects a venal and vindictive brother federal judge from a truthful and factual complaint about his extra income. A ten-year-old could figure out that if you accept gifts or income from someone you are in a position to help, you can only pretend to be neutral. Unfortunately, this principle has long ago escaped the notice of the supervisory judges of the [IDD] Circuit. They have hollowed out the appropriate ethical standards, which might inspire the confidence of principled litigants and litigators, and replaced them with rules and decisions which wink at the practice of supplementing judicial salaries with gifts and other forms of extra income from certain well-connected attorneys. The undersigned will not adopt a see-no-evil approach to judicial ethics and hopes not to be sanctioned for insisting on a higher standard.

The undersigned respectfully suggests that before he is subjected to sanction for complaining (with documentary evidence provided) about a district judge improperly maintaining a business arrangement with his former law partners - who litigate matters in his court - someone must shine a bright light into the dark corners of this federal courthouse. The Disciplinary Counsel, with a mandate to investigate lawyers who may have corrupted a federal judge, has apparently also declined to inquire - even if this is the clear line of defense of a lawyer the Disciplinary Counsel seeks to sanction.

The undersigned has been severely punished by the judge in question; he has observed the Chief Judge and the Judicial Counsel of the [IDD] Circuit turn a blind eye to documents offered in support of a complaint of misconduct. He is now required to answer ambiguous charges of misconduct for having made his complaints known to the appropriate judicial authorities by way of properly filed pleadings and properly submitted complaints of judicial misconduct. The undersigned, therefore, objects most strenuously to the prospect that he will be further punished - without any investigatory authority troubling itself to provide a truthful and straightforward answer to a very simple question:

Why should Judge [IDD], while on the bench, be permitted to enjoy gifts and income from lawyers who appear before him?

[. . .] An attorney is obligated to come forward if evidence exists that a Judge has committed a violation of the rules of judicial conduct, which raise a question about the judge's fitness to continue as a judge. Rule 8.3. of the Rules of Professional Conduct (Reporting Professional Misconduct), reads, in pertinent part, as follows:

(b) A lawyer having knowledge that a judge has committed a violation of applicable rules of judicial conduct that raises a substantial question as to the judge's fitness for office shall inform the appropriate authority.

The complained of conduct by Judge [IDD] (1) actually occurred, (2) was serious in nature and (3) raised questions about his fitness to serve as a United States District Judge. The fact that the Chief

Judge and the Judicial Counsel of the [IDD] Circuit declined to investigate Judge [IDD] - even after he violated the Judicial Complaint Rules - suggests the federal judiciary cannot supervise or correct the misbehavior of federal judges. This laxity in the face of clear evidence of misconduct does not suggest that the undersigned has acted improperly by calling attention to the misconduct.

[. . .] The Report of Magistrate Judge [IDD], the employee of Judge [IDD], is full of omissions, distortions and misrepresentations. Specifically, this Report does not state:

1. *that Judge [IDD] violated the Local Rules of his own court* in permitting his former law partner to amend a complaint without a hearing extended to the objecting adverse party.

2. Nor does the Report acknowledge the gift-giving to the judge by an organization whose President was a former law partner of the judge and *who at that time was litigating a matter before Judge [IDD]*.

3. Nor does the Report acknowledge the repeated attempts made by the undersigned by way of motions properly filed, to investigate Judge [IDD]'s misconduct and also by way of seeking a hearing before *another* federal judge; such a hearing would have included Judge [IDD]'s business relations with his former law partners; for that reason, no hearing was permitted.

4. Nor does the Report acknowledge efforts made by the undersigned, by way of pleadings properly filed, to obtain ethics guidelines which are supposed to be readily available in the chambers of every federal district judge (<u>Guide to Judiciary Policies and Procedures</u>, Vol II) but which is not made public.

Absent an examination of this volume, one can only speculate about whether Judge [IDD] was on notice that he should have disposed of his interest in property leased by a law firm whose partners and employees appeared in his court - and whom he would have wished to do well so the firm could pay him rent. (The undersigned also asked Chief Judge [IDD] for a copy of this volume; [IDD] declined to provide it.) Before the undersigned is sanctioned for proceeding in bad faith, or for some improper purpose or for harassing or vexing Judge [IDD] or the [IDD] Circuit Judicial Counsel, this document should be examined.

Nor does the Magistrate's Report state - as it should have, in order to be both candid and truthful - that Judge [IDD] had violated the Judicial Complaint rules by publishing the name of the Respondent as a <u>confidential</u> complainant.

These *deliberate misstatements of fact* by Magistrate Judge [IDD] render his Report a false, misleading and unreliable document - which served merely to provide cover for Judge [IDD]'s misconduct and also served as a fraudulent and unsound basis for the sanctioning of the undersigned - by a misbehaving federal district judge. Magistrate [IDD]'s report was apparently designed to provide a rationale for the severe sanctioning and disbarment of the undersigned while simultaneously diverting attention from Judge [IDD]'s obvious acts of misconduct.

Judge [IDD]'s documented misconduct as well as Magistrate [IDD]'s ploy in drafting a distorted Report, raise questions about the integrity and simple honesty of Judge [IDD] and Magistrate Judge [IDD]. There certainly has been interference with the proper administration of justice – but not by the undersigned.

As the undersigned argued – repeatedly but to no avail before Judge [IDD] – *a hearing before another judge* should have been conducted before sanctions were imposed. Instead, in his Order imposing sanctions, Judge [IDD] ordered that the respondent *not even be permitted to defend himself* - which might have been done by way of motions to reconsider or a motion to stay the severe sanctions imposed pending an appeal. Consequently, when the undersigned moved to stay any sanctions until an appeal had been made, this motion was returned to the undersigned by the court clerk.

A difficult, mortifying lesson has been learned by the undersigned: the [IDD] Circuit Judicial Complaint Rules are

mere words on a page and are to be taken
seriously by an officer of the court only at
great personal peril. The lawyer who relies
upon them for protection against a
vengeful judge will be punished.4 [. . .]

---

[4] The ethical standards of [IDD] Circuit judges have
been a sham for years. In an article recently taken
from the internet, [IDD], Washington Bureau
Correspondents of the [IDD] reported (Appended
Exhibit 24) in 1995 that on Dec. 6, 1988 Judge
[IDD] of the [IDD] Circuit took part in a hearing
in which the [IDD] was a litigant. In May, 1989,
Judge [IDD] received a $15,000 [IDD] from
[IDD], the [IDD] Award. He was presented the
award in a ceremony in [IDD] attended by [IDD].
Judge [IDD] said at the ceremony, "I appreciate
deeply the honor conferred upon me. I thank the
[IDD] committee . . . and, of course, [IDD]." In
September, 1989, in a decision made by [IDD]
Circuit judges - including [IDD-the gifted judge] -
a ruling was issued in [IDD-the gift giver]'s favor.
Judge [IDD] did not reveal the gift to the
litigants. His behavior subsequently was defended
by another [IDD] Circuit Judge, [IDD], who wrote
the circuit court opinion and who said it is "silly"
to think [IDD-the gifted judge] might have been
influenced by the award, because "it does not
raise a shadow of a question." Judge [IDD-the
gifted judge] took the money from [IDD], bought
a [IDD]. An appeal to the U.S. Supreme Court
went nowhere. It was subsequently reported that
three of the justices -- Byron White, William
Brennan and Sandra Day O'Connor -- had taken
lavish trips at [IDD]'s expense to meetings in

The Respondent respectfully suggests that the Board's decision must acknowledge the Judge's misconduct.

1. Judge [IDD] did indeed ignore the rules of his own court to the great benefit of this former law partners.
2. Judge [IDD] did indeed violate the Federal Rules of Civil Procedure as authoritatively interpreted by the Supreme Court.
3. Judge [IDD] did indeed accept a valuable gift from an organization presided over by a former law partner who was concurrently appearing in a matter in his own court.
4. Judge [IDD] did indeed violate the Judicial Complaint Rules of the [IDD] Circuit by ignoring the confidentiality rules of those proceedings.
5. Judge [IDD] did indeed block discovery (a proposed deposition) into matters wherein his personal financial interest were at issue.

The Hearing Committee reviewing this matter is specifically mandated to "submit to the board **written findings of fact**, conclusions of law, and recommendations, together with the record of the hearing." Please see RULE [IDD]. (Emphasis added.) Before the undersigned is subjected to the humiliation of public discipline, he must respectfully

---

[IDD], [IDD] and [IDD]. So much for judicial ethics and the required appearance of propriety.

urge that the judge's misconduct be specified in this Board's findings of fact.[5]

Furthermore, if discipline is imposed, the State Supreme Court shall issue written reasons. Please see RULES FOR [IDD] The undersigned respectfully suggests that before sanctions are imposed upon him, these proceedings must find, as matters of fact, that Judge [IDD] did indeed engage in the complained of conduct. A failure to so find will amount to both procedural and substantive unfairness to the Respondent.

Not a single one of my arguments has ever been given a response by any disciplinary or judicial authority, which has had occasion to read them. Instead of actually, honestly answering these arguments, the custodians of judicial and attorney ethics simply ignored all of it and deprived me of my ability to practice law.

---

[5] Section [IDD] of the [IDD] suggests this Board lacks the authority to review allegations of misconduct the undersigned made about a United States District Judge. The pertinent rule reads: "Full-time incumbent judges shall not be subject to the jurisdiction of the lawyer disciplinary agency." Therefore, the undersigned, prior to the filing of Formal Charges, urged the Disciplinary Counsel to examine business and tax records of *lawyers and their businesses* with whom Judge [IDD] has or had a partnership interest. The undersigned also urged this matter be referred to the United States Attorney.

The MJ made other misstatements in his Ruling, finding 29 incidents of my misconduct and recommending me for sanctions. We continue the listing of the Magistrate Judge's 29 findings and my responses to them, with number

4. threatening the court with "extra-judicial actions" (Doc 388 p. 4). As stated above (page 51) this is a reference to impeachment and to proposed changes in the law. Here follows the MJ's listing, at number 5, and following.

5. Alleging that this court has never permitted representative civil rights plaintiffs to proceed as class representatives, implying impropriety [Doc 62].

Before finding misconduct in my asking this question, why not provide an answer to it? Neither the federal court, nor the Disciplinary Counsel nor the State Supreme Court has taken the trouble to find out. First, I was blocked and then sanctioned by the judge himself and finally drummed out of the legal profession, for making this *allegation.*

6. Suggesting that the court has engaged in improper conversations with an attorney [Doc. 260].

In response to this statement, I submitted an answer (see page 126), which contained the information that I had received a call from a lawyer, who left a recorded message:

"Hey Richard, This is [IDD]. It's about 4:40 my time. Judge [IDD] gave me a call today and we had

100

a pretty good conversation. I am going to be meeting with him tomorrow afternoon. If you get a chance, call me this evening. If I am not here, leave a number where I can reach you after hours or whatever and I'll call you back. Bye."

This information was placed before both the district judge and the disciplinary counsel and, prior to charges being filed against me, before the state supreme court, who ultimately condemned me as unethical. In any fair proceeding, my *allegation* that the judge had participated in an *improper conversation*, which interfered with my efforts to secure local counsel, would need to be investigated. It was not.

*7. Suggesting that, if the court granted **a motion to which Cook, on behalf of his clients is opposed,** the courts in the [IDD] are reserved almost entirely for wealthy [predominantly white] litigants and courts and counsel need not be concerned with poor (predominantly black) plaintiffs [Doc. #309].*

This is a mischaracterization of my argument, which was simply to object to the removal of plaintiffs from their lawsuit, after demonstration had been made that efforts to locate them and keep in contact with them, had been hindered by the defendants. I also pointed out that these obstructions had been permitted by the court itself and that the court's maneuvers are so blatantly unfair, that the court may indeed be said to be reserved for well placed White litigants and their counsel, who are connected into the court. I believe this dynamic is as true today, as it was then. One way to test access by the poor to the courthouse would be to investigate whether judges, including the one presiding in this case, accept money and other gifts from lawyers and litigants, affluent enough to manage this kind of maneuver. Many such gifts are made to the bench through attorney associations. Unless forced to do so, kicking and screaming at every step, the custodians of judicial ethics, who are judges themselves and who received identical perks themselves, simply refuse to see a problem.

8. Suggesting that the court might conclude that the rape and abuse of inmates by their guards is perfectly okay. [Doc. "#309]

This court certainly had looked the other way; at the outset of this lawsuit, with several statements before it from abused women, the judge asked if it were not the case, that my clients were complaining about not getting "toothpaste" and "toothbrushes." I took this comment to be exactly what it proved to be, a signal that my clients were not going to be taken seriously. In the course of this litigation, I cited many specific instances of prisoner abuse, which the MJ stated were evidence not of judicial indifference but of my own ethical failings.

*9. **Alleging** that the court had itself contributed to the defendants' improper attempts to hijack funds.*

My attempts to interest the court in the ownership of the phone system in the jail fell on deaf ears. The phones were routinely turned off by jail personnel, when prisoners tried to call me. My investigation uncovered the fact that the phone system was at least partly owned by the son of the defendant sheriff, who was in charge of the prison. Efforts to include this company as a defendant or otherwise to make the operators of the phone system liable to the prisoners for this interference with a constitutionally protected right to communicate with counsel was ruled "irrelevant" to the lawsuit. My statement was accurate; the court had contributed to the defendant's improper efforts to hijack funds. Without acknowledging the circumstances which lead to this characterization, the Magistrate Judge finds it unethical to complain about it.

10. By filing vituperative "responses" to court orders [Doc #311 and #336]

The MJ neglects to cite the actual language he wishes to characterize as *vituperative*. The State Supreme Court takes this cue and follows suit – no one wants to look candidly at my literal language, because such an unblinking look would point too clearly at the obvious, underlying judicial misconduct, about which I was complaining.

*11. **Suggesting without support**, that the judges of the [IDD] District or in the [IDD] Circuit, "by consensus" had engaged in an effort to deny class status to civil rights plaintiffs [Doc. 311].*

I had asked for a hearing on this issue – which had never been granted. (See pages 11-13.)

*12. **Suggesting without support**, that this court had never appointed counsel to represent a prisoner in a conditions of confinement case, and* *that this court had never permitted a prisoner case to get beyond summary judgment stage **without any basis in fact**.*

I had *asked* the judge if these were the facts. My inquiry was simply ignored. A hearing on these requests was, of course, never granted. Lemming-like, an officer of the court is supposed to lead his clients off the litigation precipice, pretending that the court is going to treat his clients fairly, where there are indications to the contrary – while efforts to confirm these indications are sanctioned. If a remedial jail case in a particular court is likely to be a waste of everyone's time, why pretend otherwise?

*13. **Suggesting without support**, that complaints of prisoners about conditions of confinement are handled improperly and unfairly by this district and the court of appeal[s] [Doc 311].*

I had pointed in various pleadings to the revolving door used in this district and in this circuit, which permitted incarcerated *pro se* prisoners-plaintiffs to be ushered into court and then quickly ushered out. The travesty works like this: a handwritten prisoner complaint is received in the clerk's office. Counsel is not appointed because the matter is deemed "routine" or "uncomplicated." The prisoner is then transferred by the defendant sheriff; the jail is not required to forward her legal mail. Failing to respond to a discovery request or to some notice from the court, the case is then thrown out because the prisoner is said to have abandoned the matter, or to have missed a deadline or to have failed to respond to something or other. I had cited a number of these kinds of judicial shenanigans –

104

but my pleadings had of course been ignored. As stated earlier, these maneuvers confirm that the courts are in fact, reserved for well-paying litigants and their counsel, whose payments extend into the courthouse itself. If the MJ or the federal circuit judicial council had wanted to find out whether my complaints of judicial misconduct were merely *suggestions*, made *without support*, they could have convened a hearing and investigated them, as I had asked.

14. **Alleging** lax case management [Doc. #315]

Yes. I did allege this and documented it, pointing to such matters as (1) unwritten orders requiring me to obtain permission from the jailer before interviewing a prisoner and (2) permitting opposing counsel to go for an entire year without having to respond to discovery requests – and finding no fault in this conduct. Perhaps I could have done a better job looking after my clients' interests, had I helped pay for the court's overseas travel, gone with him, laughed at his jokes, and told him how keen were his insights as we stood together before some majestic painting. *Oh, and judge, can I take your picture with me, for the grandkids?*

15. **Alleging** the district judge's **indifference to propriety** [Doc. #315]

It is tedious to point continuously to the citing by the MJ of some *allegation* of mine, while failing to state whether the allegation is in fact the truth. I pointed out that it is improper for a federal judge to receive a gift from litigators. I also pointed out (p. 90) that my judge subsequently departed from the federal rules of civil procedure so as to grant an enormous financial benefit to the gift-giver(s). (See page 90, above.)

16. ***Suggesting*** *more than once* ***without support***, *that the district court would be amenable to accepting gifts in exchange for favorable rulings.* *[Doc. #315, #388, #399]*

This statement may be characterized as both thoroughly cynical and completely false. Once again, here is what happened, which is (1) what I reported to the Judicial Council, (2) complained about in recusal motions, (3) petitioned for a hearing to consider, (4) requested that another judge decide and (5) cited in the disciplinary proceedings brought against me:

A. My judge accepted a significant gift from an organization whose president was a former law partner of the judge and was, at the time the gift was made, simultaneously litigating a matter before the Judge;
B. this Judge violated the Local Rules of his court as well as the Federal Rules of Civil Procedure (as interpreted by the U.S. Supreme Court) by granting a motion in this matter, to amend a complaint without permitting the adverse party to respond or to participate in a hearing on the merits;
C. this Judge, contrary to the federal judicial complaint rules, identified me as a confidential complainant to the Judicial Council;
D. this Judge improperly issued orders quashing a deposition related to the inquiry into possible

improper financial dealings between this Judge and attorneys with business in his court;

E. According to a formal filing, this Judge was in a real estate partnership through which he was the landlord of his former law firm - while serving as a United Stated District Judge.

17. Suggesting, without support, *that the court had shown favoritism, to one who had "likely assisted in the advancement of the court's judicial career." [Doc. #315]*

In truth, an allegation of favoritism may not have been documented in any filings before the MJ at the time when he made his recommendations for sanctions against me. However, I had already asked for a hearing, which was never granted. At a hearing I would have attempted to prove up what I had been told by lawyers around town. I had been told that the judge's former law firm had vigorously lobbied for the appointment of the judge. I also knew that a magistrate judge, who served with this judge following his successful nomination to the bench, was from the same law firm. Thus, in a location where there is but a single federal judge and federal magistrate, both of these appointments were filled by attorneys from the same law firm – and (as I had been told) both of them received partnership payment from the law firm. In the case of the judge (not in that of the retired magistrate judge) I had been told these payments extended into his tenure on the bench. My statement that the judge had *shown favoritism* to his former law firm was truthful. The Judicial Council or the Disciplinary Counsel could have examined the relevant financial records of the law firm and the judge – an inquiry that I was barred by the judge from conducting.

*18. Attempting to engage in a **discovery expedition** with regard to the judge, the judge's wife, and the attorney involved in the issues raised in the first motion of recusal [Doc #315] when the attorney knew that **the [IDD] Circuit Court of Appeal had found no impropriety** in the judge's actions.*

Discovery expedition – this is just a way of mischaracterizing discovery requests, which are proper but which must be deemed improper to protect the judge. The MJ declined to state what actually happened to the subpoenas, seeking testimony and documents with regard to the judge, the judge's spouse, and the attorney involved. By not starting the fate of the discovery requests, the MJ does not have to admit that they were disallowed by the judge who was the subject of the discovery. According to then federal law, a federal judge is barred from ruling on matters touching his personal and private interests (page 47, above). The MJ fails to include mention of this misconduct in his 22-page Ruling. Nor do the disciplinary apparatus or the State Supreme Court Justices interest themselves in this violation – although I pointed to it in the course of the proceedings against me.

the [IDD] Circuit Court of Appeal [sic] had found no impropriety – Once again, the MJ deceives the reader. The MJ fails to specify that it was the Judicial Council, who, failing to investigate, found *no impropriety* in the judge's conduct. By declining to identify the judicial tribunal he cites, the MJ is free to ignore two embarrassments to his narrative: (1) the ruling of the Judicial Council, which he cites, was to have been held in confidence but (2) the judge, in yet another act of misconduct, made the ruling public. By failing to specify that he is talking about the Judicial Council, the MJ also saved himself from having to acknowledge that the Judicial Council declined to investigate any of my confidential complaints concerning the misconduct of the judge. No misconduct by the judge was found because the Judicial Council did nothing – except to permit the judge to violate the Council's own confidentiality rules. This Council then sat in silence on the sidelines while a State Supreme Court found misconduct in an officer of their own court for filing a confidential complaint with the Judicial Council.

19. *Suggesting that the court of appeal [sic] is **unable or unwilling to supervise the district judge** as to ethical matters [Doc. #388].*

I am happy to acknowledge the MJ's lapse into unexpected candor, in this, his 19th example of my misconduct. I agree to this characterization of my conduct. I did say that the supervising judges are unable or unwilling to undertake actual supervision of this district judge, as to matters of his misconduct. But how is it misconduct for me to point this out?

20. *Suggesting that **the court abused its official position.** [Doc. 399]*

Yes. I acknowledge this suggestion, although I would refer to my submissions not as *suggestions* but as the content of properly filed motions of recusal and confidential complaint(s).

*21. **Alleging** the court had engaged in deliberate violations of "the Judicial Complaint rules of this Circuit." [Doc. 399]*

Yes. The judge, indeed, *had engaged in deliberate violations* of these rules. No Matter. I was formally charged with making an *allegation*, which my accusers avoided admitting was true. Instead, the Magistrate Judge, in his April, 2000 Report, cited my assertion as misconduct. The judge then used this finding to justify heavy sanctions against me. The State Supreme Court then, years later, invoked the MJ's Report to justify throwing me out of the legal profession. The MJ must have thought I had invented these rules (hence, the quotation marks). But the Judicial Complaint rules do, of course, exist and are available for download and at every federal courthouse. These rules contain strictures which mandate confidentiality – a prohibition my judge brazenly ignored.

*22. Suggesting that his clients would be "sandbagged" at some future point by the court's **failure to follow the court's own rules** [Doc #399]*

If the MJ is not to be faulted for not foreseeing what was to happen, neither ought I to have been punished for foreseeing and foretelling what did happen to me and to my clients' case.

*23. Alleging that the district judge is **indifferent to the applicable judicial rules of conduct**.*

I did allege this. I argued this. I moved for recusal for this. I complained in confidence to supervising judges about this. The MJ may be excused either for not knowing of the existence of the judicial complaint rules or for having no alternative except to condemn me on pain of losing his federal appointment. But the disciplinary counsel and the state supreme courts in three jurisdictions have no such excuse. In 2000m I sent them the MJ report and recommendation, along with my responses, The three supreme courts ignored everything, except their own exquisite instinct to protect a be-robed miscreant from truthful complaints about his misconduct.

24. *Alleging* that *the judge* had used his official position to **block** an inquiry into [his] **alleged** misconduct.

In defending myself against threatened sanctions, I repeated that I had been telling the truth. Should I not have relied on the truth as a defense? I sought subpoenas for documents and for a deposition of the former managing partner of the judge's former law firm. The gist of these inquiries was to uncover instances of payments to the judge. Yet, the judge did, himself, bar this inquiry. The quashing of this discovery was certainly a misuse of his official position to block an inquiry into alleged misconduct. Perhaps the entire argument of the MJ here is based on his avoidance of a possessive pronoun: *his*, as in *his misconduct*. By failing to specify that the judge had aborted an inquiry into *his own interests*, a deceived reader might draw the conclusion that some crazy lawyer is making unsubstantiated charges about a judge's ruling on some objectified discovery request – not on discovery directed at *the judge's* relationship with lawyers appearing in his court.

25. Alleging *that the outcome of this lawsuit may be "predetermined owing to* **the venality, vindictiveness, and possible corruption** *of the tribunal." [Doc #399]*

I could not have put this better myself. In fact, this is how I did put it – and that is what happened. The only hook upon which a finding of fault may be hung upon me for these comments, is that I was not ever able to trigger an investigation into the court's financial relationships with litigators in his court. Because the Judicial Council adopted a shoot-the-messenger approach, there would never be an actual, straightforward examination of what I had complained about to the Council.

26. Alleging *that the court had* **permitted** *"flagrant abuses of judicial powers" [Doc #399]*

What I had actually said was not that the court had permitted such abuses but had engaged in them. I stand by this *allegation*.

27. *Suggesting that the judge is* **"accustomed to abusing his position by personal enrichment**." *[Doc #399]*

If a judge (1) accepts gifts, (2) departs from procedural rules so as to benefit the gift-givers, (3) is part-owner of a building housing his former law firm, which represents litigants in his court, and (4) blocks inquiries into his personal financial ties to litigators – what else can you say but this? The judge is *accustomed to abusing his position by personal enrichment.*

I am reduced to repeating a stale mantra: why did the custodians of judicial and attorney ethics conclude it was not necessary to investigate my complaints before subjecting me to a public humiliation in a forum, which, by rule, exempts judicial misconduct from its jurisdiction?

*28. By threatening that if the court attempts to impose sanctions, he will interject **alleged wrongdoing** of the court into the proceedings. [Doc #399]*

I suppose this is a reference to my stating that, if granted a hearing on sanctions, I would attempt to conduct the discovery which the judge had blocked, and that I would otherwise defend myself by renewing my assertions that the judge had violated the rules of his own court and had benefitted financially from his dealings with litigators who appear before him. I certainly would have attempted to do all of this. I certainly did tell the court this. No hearing was ever held. The court found a way to sanction and then get rid of me from this lawsuit. In their turn, the state Supreme Court Justices found a way to do the same thing – by invoking proceedings which effectively exempt the misconduct of judges from formal complaint.

*29. Making the above statements or allegations 5. through 27, without **first having made reasonable inquiry into the facts** and making the statements **in a context other than a proper motion to recuse**.*

I refer the patient reader to my responses to 5 – 28 and ask: was a *reasonable inquiry into the facts* attempted? Yes – until blocked by the judge who was the subject of all of the complaints.

The second fault found is that I made the statements *in a context other than a proper motion to recuse*. Yes. I did make statements in pleadings other than in recusal motions. Such as in confidential complaints to the Judicial Council, in motions to reconsider, in responses to show-cause orders, in motions for hearings, in arguments used to bolster motions or responses to defendant motions, such as motions to dismiss plaintiffs from the lawsuit. The MJ's catch-all condemnation ought not to have become grounds for a finding of lawyer-misconduct. Before I suffered the slightest sanction, my request that this court be investigated ought to have been honored. Instead, the judicial powers, intent on protecting one of their own at the negligible cost (to themselves) of my reputation and career, gave heed to the "report" of a posturing Magistrate Judge, himself employed as assistant to the judge about whom I had complained.

[Interview with Roc, age seven] What happens when you tell lies? *You get punished.* And if you didn't get punished, would it be naughty to tell them? *No.* I'm going to tell you two stories. There were two kiddies and they broke a cup each. The first one says it wasn't him. His mother believes him and doesn't punish him. The second one also says it wasn't him. But his mother doesn't believe him and punishes him. Are both lies they told equally naughty? *No.* Which is the naughtiest? *The one who was punished.*

Jean Piaget, *The Moral Judgment of the Child,* in *Lying: Moral Choice in Public and Private Life,* by Sissela Bok, (Vintage Books, 1979, page 77.)

CHAPTER V

NOTHING BUT RESPECT
... *NOTHING*

I continue (from page 80), with a word-for-word commentary on the State Supreme Court Order:

*Respondent **reacted** to this ruling by **reiterating his previous allegations** against Judge [IDD].*

Respondent . . . reacted [to the MJ's 4/2/00 recommendation that my complaints about the judge were grounds for sanctions] *reiterating his previous allegations* – This statement by the Justices of a State Supreme Court is breathtaking in its mischaracterization of what occurred. In fact, as the Justices knew, I had submitted a Response to the twenty-nine listed incidents of my supposed misconduct. (See below, pp. 116-35.)

In my April, 24, 2000 Response, I did not merely *reiterate previous allegations*, as the Court dismissively suggests. I certainly did repeat my fact-based allegations about the Judge's misconduct – which had never been investigated. But I also raised new matters, and new arguments. And I certainly did take this further opportunity to point out the failure of the District Court and the Judicial Council to acknowledge the judicial misconduct about which I had complained. Nor did the Judicial Council trouble to investigate my straightforward, factual recitations of that misconduct. I pointed out that all of my allegations had been submitted in properly filed pleadings and in *confidential* complaints to the supervising judges of the federal circuit court. Here is what I wrote in 2000 (excluding Exhibits) in response to the Magistrate Judge's Ruling. Five years after first receiving and ignoring it (see page 82, above), the state Justices misleadingly label this response: a repetition of *previous allegations*:

> MAY IT PLEASE THE COURT, the undersigned objects to the April 12, 2000 Memorandum Ruling of the Magistrate Judge for the following reasons.
>
> 1. The District Judge has, in fact, issued unwritten rulings in this matter, ordering telephonically that the plaintiffs may not conduct depositions of the defendants until all of the plaintiffs have been deposed.
>
> 2. Both the District Judge and the Magistrate have indicated in previous rulings that sanctions against the undersigned are contemplated. Such threats are improper because sanctions matters are to be addressed promptly. The April 4, 2000 motion is designed specifically to move this process forward. If the undersigned is to be sanctioned for making truthful statements about this Court, then any such process should be undertaken promptly and not endlessly delayed.

3. The undersigned has made no "claims" against this court. Rather the undersigned has pointed out to the Court three specific and even acknowledged violations of the Court's duties under the rules of judicial ethics and the rules of this Circuit which govern judicial complaints. The undersigned wishes to stress: there is no dispute this conduct has occurred. The only dispute is what should be done about it. As to two of the specific acts, the Judicial Counsel of the Circuit has said nothing is to be done. On behalf of my clients and myself, this outcome is unsatisfactory. I will not, without frequent protest, remain in the position of not knowing why a lawsuit was won or lost, whether on the merits of the claims made or because the judge's past conduct has indicated he is willing to accept gratuities. I do not desire to litigate a matter before a court who has (1) accepted a valuable gratuity from litigators with matters mending in the court and (2) explicitly violated a rule of the judicial circuit forbidding publication of the name of a judicial complainant. I have a higher obligation than that to my clients. What shall I tell them? You would not have lost if you had offered something to the judge? I will not be put in that position. My clients know about this dilemma and have not objected to my pursuit of a reasonable remedy, which is a recusal or transfer of this matter to another court. I shall continue to make this complaint long and

loud. The idea that I should be disbarred for telling the truth is a very dubious proposal. I do not expect to be disbarred or otherwise to be sanctioned. However, in view of the ongoing refusal of the Court to recuse himself, I do expect to secure a hearing in some venue not under the supervision of this Court. A recusal would have concluded this matter. [6]

4. The third specific act of misconduct by Judge [IDD] was the quashing of the deposition of [IDD]. Her testimony was being solicited by the undersigned with regard to any moneys, fees, rents, payments for services rendered or any other transfers of funds either to Judge [IDD] or to his wife by the [IDD] Law Firm. This inquiry was made necessary by the threat of sanctions against me by order of this Court. I will not submit to sanctions without a hearing and I will not simply show up at a hearing where my ability to conduct my profession has been placed in jeopardy. I intend to conduct discovery. After threatening me with sanctions, Judge [IDD] interfered with this deposition. A judge may not decide an action where his own interests are involved. Yet this is exactly what happened in this instance. When I attempted to take [IDD]'s deposition, Judge [IDD] himself

---

[6] Perhaps the docket entries in the [IDD] intervention in the [IDD] matter indicate how such a recusal may be facilitated.

quashed the deposition. This is improper. Judge [IDD] should have transferred this matter to another judge. 28 U.S.C. 455 states, in pertinent part:

"Any justice, judge, or magistrate of the United States shall disqualify himself in any proceeding in which his impartiality might reasonably be questioned. (b) He shall also disqualify himself in the following circumstances: [. . .] He knows that he, individually or as a fiduciary, or his spouse or minor child residing in his household, has a financial interest in the subject matter in controversy or in a party to the proceeding, or any other interest that could be substantially affected by the outcome of the proceeding; (5) He or his spouse, or a person within the third degree of relationship to either of them, or the spouse of such a person: (i) Is a party to the proceeding, or an officer, director, or trustee of a party; (ii) Is acting as a lawyer in the proceeding; (iii) Is known by the judge to have an interest that could be substantially affected by the outcome of the proceeding."

5. From records in the [IDD-Sec of State] office I know that Judge [IDD] was listed for years as the landlord of his former law firm. It is not proper for a federal judge to receive moneys from litigators. Obviously, a judge would have an interest in their success in court so they could continue to make payments to him. These payments,

if any there were, may have been made through the usual accounts receivable of the law firm or through some other mechanism such as, [IDD]. If I am going to be disbarred for truthfully stating this judge should recuse himself for the above stated conduct, I intend first to find out all that can be known about these financial arrangements.[7]

6. I know that Judge [IDD]'s wife was at some point in time engaged in some aspect of the computer software business. I believe this involvement was recent and I believe she was doing business as [IDD] Software (now defunct?), [IDD]. I also believe that her customers and/or clients included law firms, and perhaps including the [IDD] Law Firm, where Judge [IDD] was a former partner. [IDD] may also have had a business relationship with [IDD], another computer business of some kind, when this business was represented by the [IDD] Law firm and perhaps in matters before Judge [IDD] himself. I do not know if this is the case, but if I am to be disbarred, I would like to find out.

---

[7] A present or former employee of the [IDD] Law firm told me, 'If you are going to look into this, look at where Judge [IDD]'s wife gets her money.' The undersigned shall provide an affidavit or declaration, as requested, but shall provide names and dates only to another judge, not under the supervision of this Court. No one else needs to be faced with disbarment for telling the truth.

7. I deny that I have submitted any "abusive" filings or engaged in any "attacks" upon this court. What I have done is attempted, without success, to sound the alarm that the impropriety of accepting a gratuity has settled upon the undersigned a profound sense of worry. While accepting a gratuity arranged for him by an organization presided over by his former partner, Judge [IDD] then departs from the Federal Rules of Civil Procedure by granting a motion to amend a complaint, without affording opposing counsel an opportunity to offer arguments. This maneuver (I believe) led directly to a forced settlement in which his former partner and former law firm recouped something like one million dollars in fees and recoverable costs. Their client whose injuries (I believe) amounted to a suspension with pay, recovered something like six hundred thousand dollars. Only a naive simpleton would not worry that the fix is in. The obvious method of quieting these concerns is a recusal.

8. I have never heard of a judge engaging in this kind of conduct. To be confronted with it, to complain about it, to utilize the confidential complaint procedures of the Circuit, and then to be threatened vindictively, with sanctions, compounds my sense of unease. But I will not be intimidated in the slightest degree. As I told the Court when the [IDD] deposition

was quashed, if this is appropriate conduct, then there will be no need to disbar me. I will resign. Life is too short to engage in a pretence of fairness for my clients, who expect and deserve more. I will willingly submit to any kind or quality of proceeding, whether the long-threatened sanctions hearing or a disbarment proceeding - as long as the proceeding is in another court and I am permitted to defend myself through the rules of discovery.

9. I stand by everything stated in every pleading I have filed in this matter, including the December 1998 filing (Doc. 309). This court has ordered (only orally) that the plaintiffs may not depose any defendants until all of the plaintiffs are deposed. It is not incumbent upon the plaintiffs to challenge every order and every decision and they did not immediately question this one. All parties had to be deposed and the plaintiffs tried to comply. However, after attempting to comply with this procedure, for a full year, it became clear why this (unwritten) procedure was so detrimental to the plaintiffs. After a full year of making plaintiffs (some imprisoned elsewhere in the state, others 'rolled out' and back on the streets, others suffering a variety of undiagnosed mental diseases) available for their depositions, the undersigned realized the unwritten discovery scheme was but a mechanism for the dozens of plaintiffs to

state their claims while the memories of prison guards grew cold and/or they disappeared out of the area. Why had the court set us up in this manner? To find out, I began to make additional inquiries into how this court conducts his cases. By the end of 1998, I had confirmed the Court's receipt of a valuable gratuity which was accepted simultaneously with the granting of a most favorable motion to amend, permitted contrary to the applicable rule. I then promptly moved for a recusal.

10. Re. Doc. 309, this court knew the defendants refused to forward the plaintiffs' legal mail and yet has denied requests to order the defendants to do so.

11. Re. Doc 309, the plaintiffs moved this court to permit discovery into the sheriff's private business practices, after discovering the defendant sheriff was personally enriching himself by setting up a family member in a private telephone business inside the facility. The plaintiffs believe the sheriff subsequently took over this business and directly enriched himself. Yet the court ruled this self-interested conduct of a private nature was not relevant to the plaintiffs' claims that the sheriff had the phones turned off when the plaintiffs wished to call their counsel. Nor was this information relevant to the plaintiffs' claim that the sheriff had reason to be indifferent to their care. Because this

court has himself received personal enrichment by the acceptance of a valuable gratuity, the plaintiffs' counsel is reasonably concerned that this is the basis for the Court's refusal to permit inquiry into the private enrichment of the sheriff through his official position. The Court simply cannot see the problem.

12. Re. Doc 309, this court had refused the plaintiffs' requests that the defendant cease interfering with counsel's access to them and to witnesses - by permitting the imposition of a 48 hour notice requirement, thus giving plenty of time for the defendants to continue their threats and harassment.[8]

13. This lack of balance in the court's orders has not yet ceased. Although complaining about inadequate medical attention, the plaintiffs are not permitted to inquire about TB protocols in the prison - unless one of them has actually contracted TB, and can actually trace the disease to the facility. This is not the correct discovery standard, as the plaintiffs may seek to protect themselves and other prisoners against a sufficiently serious risk of future harm. The plaintiffs' complaint of medical neglect, without more, should have permitted a TB protocol inquiry.

---

[8] Please see the Accompanying Motion to Amend to Include [IDD], and its Exhibits.

14. The plaintiffs, incredibly, have been ordered not to inquire into whether the lesbian guards at the prison are permitted to cruise the dorms looking for frightened or otherwise compliant women upon whom they may gratify themselves. This is such an obvious area of gross, indeed felonious misconduct, that to overlook it suggests a malfeasant indifference not only to the well being of every prisoner in the facility but to applicable law. [9]

15. In 1998, I thought the court was unfairly limiting the normal and reasonable discovery privileges of the plaintiffs under the applicable rules; I believe so now. Having discovered this court has accepted a valuable gratuity in the past, I believed then that "wealthy white litigants" may well be favored. I believe so now. This is exactly the kind of conclusion that may be drawn from the court's failure to avoid the appearance of impropriety. The Court appears to favor some litigants over others.

---

[9] In response to the inexcusable foreclosure of this perfectly appropriate, reasonable and even essential avenue of discovery, the undersigned will seek to interest some law enforcement entity with jurisdiction to step in where this Court will not permit the plaintiffs to act to protect themselves. It is my hope that a dozen or more of the present and former ABCC guards will themselves go to prison for this misconduct.

16. Re. Doc. 311, this Court has suggested this is not a conditions case at all, but rather a case for damages, wherein each plaintiff must prove up her injuries. This is not what the plaintiffs nor their counsel contemplated nor, is it suggested, what will remedy the gross and (probably) ongoing abuses at [IDD].

17. Re. Doc 311, counsel did inquire of this Court whether the [IDD] Circuit judges had, by consensus made some kind of decision not to permit or encourage class status to civil rights litigants. At a status conference, the Court indicated no. The undersigned believes he is entitled to have asked this question. This matter went no further.

18. Re. Doc 311, the undersigned believes the Court met with attorney [IDD], after which [IDD], who had previously indicated a willingness to enroll as counsel, [IDD] has refused to respond to phone calls or letters from the undersigned. In a recorded message, left on the telephone of the undersigned, [IDD] stated,

"Hey Richard, This is [IDD]. It's about 4:40 my time. Judge [IDD] gave me a call today and we had a pretty good conversation. I am going to be meeting with him tomorrow afternoon. If you get a chance, call me this evening. If I am not here, leave a number where I can reach

you after hours or whatever and I'll call you back. Bye."

Perhaps some other "Judge [IDD]" is who [IDD] had in mind. In the event, [IDD] has not been seen or heard from again – much to the intense frustration of the undersigned who is trying to litigate this case for his clients from 1200 miles away - after the Local Affiliate of the ACLU declined to sign onto the pleadings, and direct this lawsuit, as this group had agreed to do.

19. Re. Doc. 311, this Court has declined to appoint counsel to complaining prisoners and the undersigned has complained about this. In a memorandum appended to a motion to reconsider the dismissal of five plaintiffs (including [IDD]; please see footnote 3), the undersigned wrote:

"Undersigned counsel is made uneasy by discovering, as this litigation progresses, that this Court has had opportunity in recent years to hear testimony about the jail in question but has deflected some such inquiries by denying pro se *litigants counsel and then finding a formal defect in a complaint, or in the* pro se *litigant's procedural moves, thereby rendering the* pro se *complaint ripe for dismissal. (Please see Exhibit A at pages 34, 35 and 36. and [IDD] which is not appended.)*

"In [IDD] the plaintiff (who is also a plaintiff in this litigation), was denied counsel because "the legal issues involve the application of well established and long standing principles and the factual issues are simple." (Memorandum Ruling and Order, May 24, 1996) The Magistrate Judge also found fault with the plaintiff's failure to respond to a motion for summary judgment after [IDD] stated she did not know "the next step to take."

"The idea that 1983 litigation involves "well established and long standing principles" is questionable. The conclusion that an incarcerated individual, subject to removal from one prison to another, has access to relevant materials and can apply these principles is even more questionable. Finally, the death of a prisoner/plaintiff in February, 1998, suggests that pro se complaints about this facility should be given more of a hearing then they may have received. This Court should not deflect pro se prisoner complainants away from the courthouse and also remove from ongoing litigation complainants who may be under coercion and who have managed, somehow, to get a lawyer. The plaintiffs respectfully request the above referenced individuals not be stricken at this time from the list of plaintiffs."

The five plaintiffs (including [IDD]; please see Footnote 3) were stricken anyway. The routine seems to work like this: a female prisoner at ABCC, alleging abuse, files a 1983 complaint and asks for counsel. The court denies the request for counsel and the sheriff transfers the plaintiff to another prison. The lawyer for the sheriff then moves to dismiss and the court dismisses because the prisoner is never heard from again. Case closed. The sheriff keeps making his private money and the guards keep getting prisoner for sex.

20. The Magistrate Judge implies (page 3) that I only "claimed" to represent various [incarcerated] individuals. This characterization ignores the numerous signed authorizations, which have been repeatedly placed before this court as attachments to various motions. If any signature of any plaintiff or proposed plaintiff has been omitted, it is due entirely to the clerical error of the undersigned, not to some impliedly deceitful effort of the undersigned to misrepresent his efforts to protect prisoners who, must, then, wish not to be protected. I invite this court to interview every one of the individuals who have been listed as an actual or proposed plaintiff. Indeed, before I am to be disbarred for some allegation that I have wished to represent people who never wanted my representation, I myself wish to call them to testify.

21. Re. Doc 311, the Magistrate Judge, citing Jones v. Diamond (*infra*) faults the undersigned for "without citation,

129

objecting that no hearing has been held" and stating, incorrectly, that a hearing normally is not held. On October 7, 1997 (and on other occasions) the undersigned has in fact moved to reconsider this denial, offering citations, as follows:

"This Court has dismissed the plaintiffs' various motions seeking class certification but has failed to order a hearing on any of these motions, prior to the dismissal of each of them. The failure to conduct a hearing before dismissing a motion for class certification is an abuse of discretion. [IDD - three cases cited] Therefore, the plaintiffs respectfully request this Court to reconsider its September 29, 1997 denial of class certification or assign reasons why the Court has declined to conduct a class certification hearing."

22. Re. Doc 315, the Magistrate Judge suggests that a 28 USC 144 affidavit is required to be filed in a motion seeking the recusal of the judge. This is not the case. As stated, the undersigned has attempted by means of recusal motions, to persuade the Court simply to transfer this matter without any more formalities than the transfer order itself. As the docket will attest, this is how the case arrived in this Court in the first place. Furthermore, the contemplated affidavit requires the signature of "a party" and must be brought early in the proceedings, "not less than ten days before the beginning of the term at which the

proceeding is to be heard" without good cause. The undersigned is unaware of any reason to think there might have been "a personal bias or prejudice" in 1995. The gratuity which has caused the appearance of impropriety was not offered or accepted until (it is believed) 1997. The unwritten orders and the failure to convene hearings occurred subsequently.

23. Re Doc 315. The undersigned affirms that it is the case that only in December, 1998, did he confirm what he had heard in April 1998. In April, 1998, and throughout 1998, the undersigned was attempting to accommodate himself to the (unwritten) orders of the court concerning depositions. The undersigned was not looking for reasons to attack this judge. Only some months later did it become apparent how unfair it was for his clients to be faced with such unwritten orders. Only then did the undersigned decide to pursue any allegations or, indeed, rumors of impropriety - in an effort better to understand why this case was almost three years old and yet the plaintiffs had not been permitted to conduct a single deposition. This investigation was undertaken because of the accumulation of "idiosyncrasies" as outlined in the recusal motion: a failure to notice an important motion for hearing, the issuance of oral orders, which are not subsequently memorialized in writing, the failure to conduct a hearing before denying a motion

seeking class representation. Finally, it was only at the end of 1998 that the undersigned learned that the trip in question was actually facilitated by a litigator in Judge [IDD]'s court, who *was on the committee in question, president of the attorney group in question,* and a former law partner of the judge as well as presently litigating a matter before the Judge. The undersigned continues to believe the offering and accepting of a valuable gratuity under these circumstances is inherently improper as, at the least, a failure to avoid the appearance of impropriety. It is for this reason that the undersigned is seeking to review those ethical guidelines, which are available to every district judge but which, interestingly, are not made public. The undersigned does not believe there exists any authority whatsoever, whether formal directive or informal recommendation, which sanctions the acceptance of such a gratuity under such circumstances. The plaintiffs are not in a position to offer a European trip to this Court. By accepting the same while simultaneously greatly assisting a trip-giver by signing an order to amend the trip-givers complaint, the Court suggests that things go better for the connected, the favored, the lawyers with an inside track to the court. This is precisely what the appearance of an impropriety is all about. And it is offensive.

24. The Magistrate Judge, lacking in candor, fails to note that the publication of the identity of the undersigned as a judicial complainant is an explicit violation of the rules governing judicial complaints. This lapse suggests that the Magistrate Judge, an employee of the Court, who serves at his pleasure, and whose rulings have no independent authorization, is unable objectively to review this matter. An explicit rules violation should be acknowledged. If not, this Memorandum Ruling is but an exercise designed to excuse the misconduct of an already enormously powerful judicial entity. If the enforcement of the rules and the sanctions for their violation are only aimed at the powerless and the complainants, while the powerful can manipulate them with impunity then, as stated, this Court will not have to trouble itself to disbar me. I have no desire to be part of such a profession. In the meantime, however, I renew my request to see what is contained in Volume II of the <u>Guide to Judiciary Policies and Procedures.</u>

25. Confidential judicial complaints are now at issue in a disbarment proceeding. However, before the Magistrate Judge states that the [IDD] Circuit Judicial Counsel concluded that Judge [IDD] "acted properly" he should read each of the rulings in question. Is he permitted to do so? Who is likely ever to come forward in the future in complaint of a judge?

133

26. As correctly highlighted by the Magistrate Judge, the undersigned does indeed believe the [IDD] Circuit is unable and/or unwilling to supervise the ethical conduct of the district judges, as evidenced in this instance. For this reason, the undersigned is pursuing an "extra-judicial" remedy, i.e., a change in the law, and has communicated with the Senate Judiciary Committee. There should be non-judges (indeed, non-lawyers) involved in the judicial complaint process. The undersigned doubts if any person who has read to this point could find an individual in the country (except a lawyer or another judge) who would think it OK for a judge to accept a gift arranged for by a bunch of lawyers or by a lawyer appearing in his court. The response would likely be, at the very least, 'it does not look good.' The undersigned respectfully suggests that judges, meeting and deciding such matters alone, may be unable to reach this conclusion. The undersigned further speculates that one or more of the judges on the Judicial Counsel may have themselves accepted a similar gratuity and therefore, may be hesitant to sanction conduct that they themselves have at engaged in. Before I am disbarred, I hope to find out.

The undersigned specifically denies that he has engaged in any conduct involving dishonesty, fraud, deceit, or misrepresentation.

Thus did I respond on April 24, 2000 to the MJ's recommendation that I be sanctioned. This Response was ignored by the miscreant federal judge, who issued an Order on June 30, 2000 requiring me to pay $7,500 into the court and suspending me from representation of my clients until the fine was paid. The rationale for the fine was as follows:

*"The Court has reviewed the pleading filed by counsel for the plaintiffs in response to the court's rule to show cause dated 31 May 2000. Attorney Richard B. Cook is fully aware of the transgressions in contravention to orders from this court concerning discovery into areas that the court has ruled are off-limits and immaterial to this particular lawsuit. **No ameliorating explanation of consequence** is given for the obvious infractions."*

no explanation of consequence - This is a false statement. Specifically (see pages 117-18, items 3 and 4), I had stated the following:

"The undersigned has pointed out to the Court three specific and even acknowledged violations of the Court's duties under the rules of judicial ethics and the rules of this Circuit which govern judicial complaints. The undersigned wishes to stress: there is no dispute this conduct has occurred. [. . .] I do not desire to litigate a matter before a court who has (1) accepted a valuable gratuity from

135

litigators with matters mending in the court and (2) explicitly violated a rule of the judicial circuit forbidding publication of the name of a judicial complainant. [. . .]

"The third specific act of misconduct by Judge [IDD] was the quashing of the deposition of [IDD]. Her testimony was being solicited by the undersigned with regard to any moneys, fees, rents, payments for services rendered or any other transfers of funds either to Judge [IDD] or to his wife by the [IDD] Law Firm. This inquiry was made necessary by the threat of sanctions against me by order of this Court. [. . .] After threatening me with sanctions, Judge [IDD] interfered with this deposition. A judge may not decide an action where his own interests are involved. Yet this is exactly what happened in this instance. When I attempted to take [IDD]'s deposition, Judge [IDD] himself quashed the deposition. This is improper.

"Judge [IDD] should have transferred this matter to another judge. 28 U.S.C. 455."

Gift giving - probably the most dynamic of all social arts"
Gwyn Thomas
A Few Selected Exits, Page 83

CHAPTER VI

**BUEN VIAJE,
SEÑOR JUEZ!**

As stated, the miscreant federal judge
characterized my response (pages 116-35, above) as
"no explanation of consequence." In their turn, the
state Supreme Court ignored the information I had
made available just as they had ignored all evidence
of the judge's misbehavior. Instead, the Justices
describe all of my arguments as a recitation of
previous allegations. (See above, pages 80, 115.)

This characterization is false and misleading.
The error is compounded by the failure of the Court
to investigate the issues raised before announcing
me to the world as an unethical lawyer - for having
insisted on an honest judge. Instead, the Justices
cruise at full throttle, finding yet more misconduct
in me, while avoiding both the actual facts and the
precedents, which I cited. The Justices state:

*Respondent never appealed the denial of his
clients' motions to recuse. Instead, he
continued to reiterate his allegations against Judge
[IDD] and later **added allegations against
Magistrate Judge [IDD]**. He also continued to
raise **the issue of deposing [IDD]**.*

137

Respondent never appealed the denial of his clients' motions to recuse [. . .] added allegations against Magistrate Judge [. . .] the issue of deposing [IDD]. The Supreme Court Justices add to their sum of my misdeeds these three additional acts. They simply ignore the fact that the formal charges leveled against me - as fuzzy as they were – make no mention of a failure to file an appeal as ethical misconduct. The Justices decline to indicate when an appeal of a judge's order is required by the rules of professional conduct and when the failure to appeal becomes misconduct. Nor do they specify the conduct of the Magistrate Judge, which in fact might have warranted a recusal (once again, characterizing as *allegations* my statements of actual fact).

*His **allegations** of misconduct against Judge [IDD] **continued up to and including the formal hearing in this matter**.*

allegations continued up to and including the formal hearing in this matter – Yes. I never ceased pointing out that I had been telling the truth. This statement is cited as a "finding" rather than a fact. The Justices viewed my insistence upon the truth of my statements as nothing more than additional evidence of bad behavior.

*Based on these findings, the hearing committee determined that respondent violated Rules 3.1, 4.4, and 8.4(d) of the Rules of Professional Conduct. Respondent **did not pursue the proper review of Judge [IDD]'s rulings through interlocutory appeal**. Instead, he continued to pursue the same issues to the point of obsession and* *in a **vexatious manner**. Furthermore, despite having notice that [IDD] and [IDD], who were not parties to the [IDD] suit, objected to his subpoenas, respondent attempted to obtain the information through [IDD]'s deposition.*

did not pursue the proper review of Judge [IDD]'s rulings through interlocutory appeal [. . .] a vexatious manner [. . .] through deposition. It came as a surprise to learn that a failure to file an appeal can be grounds for discipline – even when no notice of this failure was cited as misconduct in formal charges. The Justices here refer to my *vexatious manner*.

Truthful complaints of judicial misconduct might well seem *vexatious* to a miscreant judge. Continuing with an avoidance strategy so as to keep well away from having to acknowledge that I was telling the truth all along, the Justices fail to acknowledge what had gone on in that court. Instead, they select a pejorative adjective and apply it to a lawyer who blew the whistle on judicial misconduct. In this way the Justices are able to assign fault to my efforts to discover the extent of the district court's financial ties to litigators. Yet again, the Justices fail to acknowledge that I had first asked the supervising judges of the federal Circuit to protect an officer of their own court from a venal, misbehaving jurist whose ethical conduct is their responsibility.

Respondent's conduct as a whole amounted to conduct prejudicial to the administration of justice.** The committee determined that respondent knowingly engaged in **disruptive conduct** in the [IDD] case. However, **his

behavior was not intended to personally benefit himself or his clients. The committee agreed with [IDD], who felt that respondent believed what he was doing was right but allowed his cause to become a crusade.

Respondent's conduct as a whole amounted to conduct prejudicial to the administration of justice. It is unfair when a lawyer subject to discipline is condemned for *conduct as a whole.* No doubt, any judge with his/her hand in a litigator's pocket will be relieved to learn of this new theory: a judge on the take does not engage in *conduct prejudicial to the administration of justice* but a lawyer who complains about this kind of judge, has his reputation and his ability to earn a living thrown away for his *conduct as a whole.*

disruptive conduct – Someone who raises the alarm when seeing a thief making off with a car ought not to be cited for *disruptive conduct* for calling the police. The only people likely to reason this way are other thieves.

behavior not intended to personally benefit himself or his clients – I suspect my motives would have been better appreciated – and winked at like the motives of the lawyers who give money gifts to judges – if it had been shown that I had actually tried to benefit myself or my clients. My abused clients and I ought to have snuggled into the familiar *gift-to-me, ruling-for-you* vortex, which is the apparent judicial norm. The Justices do not know what to do with a lawyer, who blows the whistle on the money-for-ruling gift exchange, except throw him out of the "profession."

believed what he was doing was right but allowed his cause to become a crusade – All of this is merely a characterization, not a clear and convincing specification of actual behavior. What was my so-called mistaken belief? That judges really are permitted to bend the rules of their own court to enrich a gift giver and a business partner? That despite the judicial complaint rules, it is a grave error to make a confidential complaint about a miscreant judge? At what point must an officer of the court not permit a *cause* to become a *crusade* – when it becomes clear that your clients' matter is lost because your judge awards rulings to gift givers and you have failed to get into that game?

In mitigation, the committee also placed significant weight on a report of respondent's psychotherapist, who indicated that respondent's response to **perceived injustices** *resulted in obsessive behavior, which opinion is consistent with the evidence in the record.*

  perceived injustices – These references are to a letter from a therapist, whom I had begun to visit shortly after my withdrawal from the jail case. Unable to find a venal motive for my denunciations of a federal judge, the committee sought a pretext for drumming me out of the legal profession. They settled on a psychological one: an obsessive reaction to *perceived* injustice. It may or may not be a therapist's task to determine actual facts but that ought to be the clear duty of a professional disciplinary process. Ignoring this responsibility, the Justices of a state Supreme Court were content to describe my perception of the misdeeds of my judge as aberrant. They did not trouble themselves to establish if my perception was caused by the judge's *actual misconduct*. Of course, my perception was of a concrete injustice, a series of them: the judge had done exactly what I had said he did. And had gotten away with it.

THE DISCIPLINARY COMMITTEE

The professional affiliations of the three-member disciplinary hearing committee raised questions about their objectivity. One was not a lawyer, but lived in or near the community where the judge also lived. The other two members of the committee were both lawyers. The firm of at least one of them was actively practicing before the miscreant judge. Worse: *both of the lawyers on the disciplinary committee were members of the attorney organization that I had complained about for having sent my judge on a European holiday.*

Ask yourself: how likely would it be for these lawyers to conclude that the judge had engaged in misconduct or that their own attorney association had done so for having facilitated the gift? If these attorneys had found improper conduct by the judge or by their own organization, this would have meant the end of their law careers.

A chimpanzee could be trained to blow a whistle when members of an organization that gave money to a judge are convened to decide if the money gift was improper. Chimp, tell the Justices: you need to recruit someone else to make that call – not the people who had given the gift.

The venue for the disciplinary hearing was improper. I had objected to the venue (the community where the court was seated) on procedural grounds because the disciplinary committee did not follow the written rules for venue. In essence, the committee ought to have been composed of lawyers who did not practice before the miscreant judge; the hearing ought to have been conducted in another part of the state. Why? By rule, a disciplinary matter is supposed to be adjudicated where the alleged misconduct took place. In my case, both the formal charges and all of the added-in charges had to do with pleadings filed and also with my confidential complaints to the federal circuit judicial council. Both the pleadings and the confidential complaints had been formally filed before a clerk of court whose office was elsewhere. I asked how the venue was selected, in violation of the written procedural rules and I requested a transfer of venue.

My motion received a one-word response from the lawyer/chairman of the disciplinary committee: DENIED. The reasons given in response to my objections to the venue may be read in this little box.

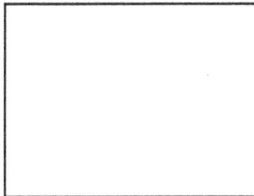

The Court's decision once again:

Under these circumstances, the committee recommended that respondent be suspended for three years. **Neither respondent nor the ODC filed an objection to the hearing committee's recommendation.**

I did not object to the committee's recommendation. I had already objected (see above pp. 116-35) in April, 2000, to any efforts to punish me and again, after the ODC wrote to me in Dec, 2002. I asked the DC to conduct a thorough investigation before charging me with anything. I submitted additional objections in response to formal charges (above, pp. 85-99) and, yet again, in copious submissions prior to and during the disciplinary committee hearing, in August, 2004.

In all of this:

- I had submitted dozens of pages of pleadings, arguments, exhibits, factual statements and legal arguments.
- I had insisted both on my veracity and upon the fact that neither I nor any lawyer ought to be drummed out of the legal profession for making truthful, confidential complaints about the misconduct of a federal district judge.
- I had complained about the venue, which had placed this matter in the hands of lawyers who were members of the organization that had arranged for the gift to the judge. Had this organization also sent the Circuit Judges travelling? What about the Justices of the state Supreme Court?
- I believed then and believe now that any objection I might have made subsequent to the findings and the recommendations of the disciplinary committee would merely lead to the re-writing of their findings, without any real likelihood of a reversal. After all, I still had not given any money to a judge.
- Any further objection stood little change of prompting an investigation of the judge. This had not happened thus far and my defense had to do with the misconduct of a judge. But a

judge's conduct falls outside the jurisdiction of the attorney disciplinary proceedings.

- The Disciplinary Board and also the Supreme Court Justices had the file. They could investigate and reverse all of this without additional and redundant paperwork from me.
- The Justices' earlier decrees in disciplinary matters announced that they considered afresh the record "below." Any appeal I might make would simply reiterate what I had already placed on the record.
- An appeal involves additional heavy costs – when you lose – and I had already lost. I knew I would have to pay for additional time expended by the disciplinary counsel and for his travel to attend the meeting of the disciplinary board. All of this would be multiplied, should I object, yet again, before the state Supreme Court.
- Just let it go until my public banishment from the legal fraternity – for complaining about judicial misconduct – may be evaluated by persons who are not in the habit of passing money to a judge.

Disciplinary Board Recommendation

After reviewing this matter, the disciplinary board determined that the hearing committee's findings of fact are **not manifestly erroneous**.

not manifestly erroneous - It ought to have been manifest on the record that there is something gravely amiss when a lawyer makes a confidential, truthful complaint to supervising judges about a miscreant federal judge – and has his career thrown away for this. It ought to have been manifest on the record that the findings of misconduct had nothing to do either with the formal, written charges or with the added-in charges, after the formal charges disappeared from view.

*The **board** also determined that respondent violated the Rules of Professional Conduct as alleged in **the formal charges**. Specifically, the board found that **instead of proceeding with interlocutory appeal of the denial of the motion to recuse**, respondent continued to "**tirelessly**" pursue **the issue** at the district court level **without a good faith legal basis to do so**.*

the formal charges – The formal charges (see page 37) made no mention of a failure to file an appeal. This sin was smuggled in after the formal charges had been filed against me.

instead of proceeding with interlocutory appeal of the denial of the motion to recuse – As noted (page 139), I was never formally charged with failing to appeal and I should not have been. As I had pointed out in earlier pleadings, my judge had suspended me from appearing further in the case and my pleadings were not filed by the clerk but were returned to me. Furthermore, as I pointed out in a pleading filed before I was gagged, an immediate appeal of such an order is untimely. *Richardson-Merrell, Inc. v. Koller* 472 U.S. 424, 449-331 (1985) (orders disqualifying counsel in a civil case are not collateral orders subject to immediate appeal as final arguments).

The characterization of my conduct as devoid of a *good faith legal basis* and *a tireless* pursuit of "the issue" takes no account of my legal arguments or the authorities I cited or of my need to respond to court orders such as an order to show cause why I ought not be sanctioned.

the issue at the district court level - What was *the issue* which I had pursued *in bad faith* and about which I ought to be stricken from the attorney roles?

* My punishment for having properly filed a recusal motion, truthfully complaining of judicial misconduct?
* A second such motion based on further judge misconduct?
* The refusal of higher judicial authority to investigate the judge?
* The public exposure and condemnation by the subject judge of myself, for having filed a confidential complaint with the Judicial Council?

Take your choice. The underlying *issue* was the undisputable misconduct of a United States District Judge. This was the *issue* other federal judges, the office of the Disciplinary Counsel and the Justices of a state's highest court concentrated their energies upon ignoring. Black's Law Dictionary might cite my prosecution as an example of *bad faith* – by the bench.

Why are the circuit judges and the state supreme court Justices not obligated to admit that a lawyer, whom they are throwing out of the profession, was telling the truth about a judge? When must an officer of the court stop telling the truth? When do you throw in the towel and admit that in court, reporting judicial misconduct is as welcome as road kill?

Furthermore, respondent's pursuit of discovery from **third persons not involved in the [IDD] case** *was burdensome to these parties.*

third persons not involved in the [IDD] case – If a federal judge has been corrupted by a gift, as evidenced by his bending the rules of his own court, this judge is unfit to preside in any matters important to my clients or anyone else's clients. This principled position is called *misconduct.* I discovered judicial shenanigans and complained about them. The supervising judges did nothing, except to permit the judge to fine me $7,500 and banish me from his court. In light of their failure to investigate, I sought documents and information from *third persons,* which might demonstrate the financial ties of the judge to litigators in his court. This discovery attempt was deemed improper.

Why would a state Supreme Court fault my efforts to obtain this information and overlook (1) the failure of the supervising judges to investigate and (2) the judge himself quashing subpoenas that are directed at uncovering his own financial ties to litigators in his court? Why would the Justices pass over all of this and condemn a lawyer who blew the whistle? Where is the analysis that supports this reasoning? Where are their authorities?

Let the Justices themselves come clean about the extent of their enrichment by lawyers who practice in the system over which these Justices preside. Do they travel on the nickel of practitioners who appear before them? Do they benefit personally from the gifts of lawyer associations, whose members' income depends upon favorable outcomes in courts under their supervision?

*Respondent's conduct caused **undue expense** and effort in the federal court proceedings and also caused the defendants to accrue extra expenses.*

undue expense —It would be interesting to know what this undue expense included. Did I cost this judge a future trip or two? Did my judge miss out on another European holiday because of the public nature of the disciplinary proceedings used against me? If gift-giving to the court is perfectly proper, then let there be transparency about who is gifting the judges. Where in the courthouse are the records kept that itemize the gifts? Who makes the offer? Is the offer made to the judge by letter? By phone? Is it the phone in the chambers of the judge? in the clerk's office? Or is it to a personal cell phone? Where are the telephone logs which might identify the person who receives the offer? Who accepts the offer? Is it the judge, in person? Is there bargaining? Is some of this the role of the court clerk? of a law clerk? a secretary? Does the offer come to the judge at home? Over lunch? Over dinner? Must the offer never come from someone with a current case before the judge, or does that not matter at all? Are the funds paid over into a personal account? Into a court account? To a travel agency? Are incidental expenses included? How about the cost of entertainment for the judge or the judge's companion(s)? Is the judge's credit card bill paid? Is the judge reimbursed? In cash? Does the court clerk or the judge maintain special accounts or credit cards, which are used for these sorts of arrangements? Is any of this reported as income? Is it reported at all? To anyone?

Based on these findings, the board determined that respondent knowingly, if not intentionally, **violated a duty owed to the legal system,** *causing* **significant harm** *to the federal courts as well as [IDD], [IDD], and the defendants in the [IDD] case.*

> *violated a duty owed to the legal system –* Apparently the *duty owed* has nothing to do with following the judicial complaint rules or with telling the truth. Do these lesser duties still exist? What about the judicial complaint rules? Following them gets you disbarred. What about the truthful substance of a motion of recusal? What is the unspecified *duty owed to the legal system*, which trumps those faded values, truth and integrity? Should I have known I might have avoided all of this by acknowledging an unwritten *duty owed to the legal system*: kick in for a judicial trip?
> *significant harm –* How is it harmful for a judge to be told he ought not bend the procedural rules of his own court in order to help a pal? How is it harmful to attempt (an attempt blocked by the subject judge) to ask the former managing partner of a law firm if there is information, which documents a judge's financial ties to litigators in his court? Why is the judge himself allowed to rule on discovery directed at his own interests, in violation of the canons of judicial ethics? Why do the Justices of the state Supreme Court overlook all of these matters in order to find fault with an officer of their own court, who refuses to look the other way?

Relying on the ABA's Standards for Imposing Lawyer Sanctions, the board determined that the baseline sanction is a period of suspension. As

aggravating factors, *the board identified a pattern of misconduct and refusal to acknowledge the wrongful nature of the conduct.*

    a pattern of misconduct – There was a pattern of misconduct. Where we differ is whether this was attorney or judicial misconduct. I believe now that at the outset of the proceedings against me, the Disciplinary Counsel and the Justices knew they could not dare find a pattern of misconduct by a federal judge. No, they best find misconduct in the lawyer who complained about the judge. We can all admire their rigorous loyalty, but not their willingness to leverage the truth in order to forge an imaginary portrait of a lawyer out of control.

    a refusal to acknowledge the wrongful nature of the conduct – My insistence that I had done nothing wrong is taken as evidence of guilt, an *aggravation* to the Justices. The odor of this logic rises familiar off the page: an admission of guilt is always preferred by the Inquisitor. You will be punished further if you insist that you have done nothing wrong. This pantomime of an actual, in depth inquiry meets you and slaps you down, when you mull over the false choice of an appeal to the very Justices who set up this disciplinary apparatus – which exempts them from any scrutiny of their own behavior. An appeal would just *aggravate* the Justices.

As mitigating factors, it found the absence of a prior disciplinary record, **personal or emotional problems,** *full and free disclosure to the disciplinary board and a cooperative attitude toward the proceedings,* **inexperience in the**

151

practice of law (*admitted 1992*), *and imposition of other penalties or sanctions.*

personal or emotional problems . . . *inexperience in the practice of law* – Insisting that your judge not be on the take is not considered a commendable quality to these Justices but a *problem* of personal or emotional dimension in the lawyer. The deliberate, permanently demeaning aspect of this comment is matched to the logic of character assassination inherent in the decree as a whole. The lesson here, administered publicly as a caution to all practitioners is this: an attorney, tempted to complain confidentially about a judge who accepts gifts from litigators and who does favors in return, is on notice that such complaints will be characterized as some sort of personal or emotional problem.

What does judicial greed for gifts from litigators suggest about the emotional state of the judge who is on the take? Is venality an emotional problem? Is it suggestive of a lack of fitness for the bench? What about dishonesty in the Justices in misstating the facts and overlooking the actual charges in their judicial decision, which destroys the reputation of an officer of their own court? What about the refusal to investigate allegations of judge misconduct? All of this might be seen as evidence of some sort of disorder in be-robed authority, which indulges itself by casually signing off on this rubbish.

It is rubbish, notwithstanding the signatures of the judges on the federal circuit and the Justices of a state's highest court. They are all fixated on protecting a miscreant on the bench, who misuses his constitutionally protected position to punish properly filed, factual complaints directed at his own misconduct. The other judges come to the aid of the miscreant because they have too much at stake. The free trips to Europe, or to the Gulf Coast and the ski resorts and the hunting lodges are too pleasurable to give up. Since the judges themselves decide what conduct creates even an appearance of impropriety, they do not have to give them up.

When it comes to gifting judges, *Don't Ask Don't Tell* is the wrong approach. The gifting of judges should either be embraced with attendant transparency and oversight or the practice should be forbidden.

My *inexperience in the practice of law* never came up (in my recollection) in any context and I reject this characterization. It is announced by the Justices ostensibly as an aspect of mitigation of my punishment. In fact, it is intended to demean me and to further blacken my reputation. I was never asked to document my expertise. Had I been asked to do so, I would have pointed to various matters of representation, including my work in immigration courts in at least four states and my record of having obtained political asylum for approximately 95% of my clients. (The national average is about 20% and probably has dropped further in the last few years.) I would place this litigation record against that of any of the Justices, who condemned me – before they switched from one end of the money spigot to the other and then signed off on the public assassination of my character. All of my work for indigent, terrified, suffering individuals was brought to an ignoble end by the court's Decree, as intended.

A person who declines to look away when confronted with the practice of gifting judges is not someone these Justices want to see running around with a law license. Never having been asked about it, I read of my *inexperience* in a decree, which is recorded as a public, permanent and unassailable statement of fact. To so characterize an officer of their court brings shame upon any set of judges, who would countenance or publish this mischaracterization – all to protect a judge accused of misconduct, whom they decline to investigate.

*Turning to the issue of an appropriate sanction, the board looked to this court's prior jurisprudence and determined that the three-year suspension recommended by the hearing committee is too harsh. Like the attorneys in [IDD], [IDD], and [IDD] respondent filed repetitive and unwarranted pleadings in ongoing litigation. Also, like Stratton, respondent's **frivolous and harassing claims** and requests for discovery burdened third persons.*

frivolous and harassing claims –It is not just frogs who repeatedly jump into the same pond. Here, the Justices line up on the edge and fling themselves in yet again. *Rib-bit!* They cannot get enough of this muck. All of this, as I have pointed out repeatedly (because the Justices repeat their misstatements), without any attempt to get to the bottom of what I had said my judge actually did.

The *claims* I had made which were previously called mere *allegations* (below, pages 21-23, 33, 41, 45, 55-56, 59-60, 80-83, 101, 112-13, 115, 137-48) are now declared to be *frivolous* AND *harassing* – as if someone had actually investigated them.

However, the board found that respondent's conduct and the resulting harm were not as egregious as that found in the three cited cases.

154

*Furthermore, respondent's **conduct spanned approximately three years,** which was considerably less than the ten-year spans in [IDD] and [IDD]. Respondent also did not cause direct harm to his clients as did [IDD] and [IDD]. Taking these circumstances into account, as well as the numerous mitigating factors present, the board determined that it is appropriate to defer eighteen months of a three-year suspension.*

conduct spanned approximately three years – The three-year span of my misconduct apparently is calculated from June, 26, 1998, with the filing of a pleading, which the Court had earlier described (page 70) as a *first sign of trouble.* Even with this date in mind, you only get to 21 months before I was removed from the case in March, 2000. No matter. And no matter, either, that no charge was ever brought, which alleged any impropriety in the June 26, 1998 filing. Yet, the pleading is trotted out twice by the Justices as evidence of misconduct serious enough to justify my public condemnation.

*Accordingly, the board recommended that respondent be suspended from the practice of law for three years, with all but eighteen months deferred. **Neither respondent nor the ODC filed an objection** to the disciplinary board's recommendation.*

Neither respondent nor the ODC filed an objection – I have indicated (pages 145-46) why an objection to the committee's recommendation seemed to me very much of a false choice – not least because of the precedent of the Justices themselves, to view an insistence upon actual innocence as an aggravating factor. In the lunatic world of attorney discipline, where a lawyer is driven from the profession for complaining truthfully about judicial misconduct, it is no surprise that a failure to confess is taken as a refusal to admit to wrong-doing.

The Court toodles on:

DISCUSSION

*Bar disciplinary matters come within the original jurisdiction of this court. [IDD] Consequently, **we act as triers of fact and conduct an independent review of the record to determine whether the alleged misconduct has been proven by clear and convincing evidence**. In re [IDD]. While we are not bound in any way by the findings and recommendations of the hearing committee and disciplinary board, we have held **the manifest error standard is applicable to the committee's factual findings**. See In re [IDD].*

we act as triers of fact and conduct an independent review of the record to determine whether the alleged misconduct has been proven by clear and convincing evidence – In light of the failure by the Justices to investigate the truth of my statements about judicial misconduct, these comments are no more than self-congratulatory jargon; they are asides, tossed off on the way to a pre-determined execution. No actual facts were put to trial. No independent review was conducted. My alleged misconduct was taken as proven by the mere citation to it, with an avoidance of quoting from my own, factual statements, or analyzing the authorities I cited in their support. The charade, not the

156

evidence marshaled against me, is clear if not convincing.

*We find **the record supports the hearing committee's factual findings**, and that respondent violated the Rules of Professional Conduct as alleged in the formal charges. Respondent filed **repetitive and unwarranted pleadings** in ongoing litigation. He also made **frivolous and harassing claims for discovery against third persons not involved in the litigation.***

the record supports the hearing committee's factual findings – As stated, the one fact, the import of which is tenaciously avoided, is that I was telling the truth. Everyone involved in my prosecution settled on a fact-avoidance stratagem. This enabled the disciplinary authorities to tiptoe around what the judge did and to find a way to punish me for refusing to do so.

repetitive and unwarranted pleadings – Which were these again? The recusal motions, which were supported by undisputed facts and authorities? The *confidential* complaint to the Judicial Council, publicized by the subject judge? Motions seeking a hearing before sanctions were imposed? Why do the Justices fail to specify exactly which of my many pleadings they find *repetitive and unwarranted?* This kind of specificity would mire them in the muck of the gifting of judges. This degree of precision would require them to observe that the Formal Charges against me focused on a recusal motion and a confidential complaint – when in fact, nothing could be found wrong with these filings. In their Decree, the allegation of misconduct for having submitted a confidential complaint to the Judicial Council of a federal Circuit has disappeared from view – because there had never been anything remotely improper in the filing of it. Rather than dismissing this charge, it is ignored by the Justices, tossed into the outer darkness, with the complaint and the lawyer who filed it, but who first must be found unethical on other grounds.

frivolous and harassing claims for discovery against third persons not involved in the litigation – I would suppose that most discovery requests may be viewed as *harassing* and perhaps *frivolous* by the party to whom the discovery is directed. Frequently, such information is in the possession of a witness, who is not in any way involved in the litigation. This is so routine it hardly requires notice – except that here it is cited as misconduct to make an inquiry.

To condemn me for seeking information and financial records, after filing a confidential complaint of judicial misconduct to supervising judges, begs an answer to a question the Justices will not address: *why did the supervising federal judges on the Circuit not themselves gather this material?*

To find it unethical of me to attempt to seek information to be used in my defense against a sanctions threat made by a miscreant federal judge raises a host of questions, which hang over this travesty like moss shrouding a cypress swamp:

- Why should the misconduct of a federal judge be papered over by state supreme court justices?
- Why should this federal judge be permitted to block an inquiry into his financial ties to litigators in his court?

- Why should supervising judges place this judge beyond the reach of the canons of judicial ethics?
- Why should a lawyer and an officer of the court be forbidden to protect himself by inquiring about this judge's financial ties to litigators in his court – and at the same time condemned for failing to uncover the facts when filing a complaint about judicial misconduct?
- Why is the issue of the misconduct of a federal judge placed in a state disciplinary proceeding which, by rule, bars inquiry into the behavior of judges?

These matters were raised in filings I made in connection with the disciplinary proceedings invoked against me. No specific response was made to any of this. The Justices announced they had fulfilled their duty, which was to *conduct an independent review of the record* of the proceedings of the disciplinary committee and the board. Finding no fault with these proceedings, they conclude:

Having found evidence of professional misconduct, we now turn to a determination of the appropriate sanction for respondent's actions. In considering that issue, we are mindful that **disciplinary proceedings are designed to maintain high standards of conduct, protect the public, preserve the integrity of the profession, and deter future misconduct**. *[IDD]. The discipline to be imposed depends upon the facts of each case and the seriousness of the offenses involved considered in light of any aggravating and mitigating circumstances. [IDD].*

disciplinary proceedings are designed to maintain high standards of conduct, protect the public, preserve the integrity of the profession, and deter future misconduct – None of these four principles can be taken seriously. What *high standard of conduct* has been maintained by overlooking judicial shenanigans involving money gifts and favors? How is *the public protected* by throwing out of the legal profession an attorney, who denounced a misbehaving federal judge? What *integrity* has this exercise *preserved*? Just what *future misconduct* will be deterred? Well, they have a point. Having announced that it is misconduct when a lawyer comes forward with properly filed complaints of actual judicial misbehavior, there will be a lot less of this sort of aberrant complaining in the future.

Respondent knowingly violated a duty owed to the legal system, causing significant harm to the federal courts as well as others. The baseline sanction for this misconduct is suspension. The aggravating and mitigating factors found by the board are supported by the record. The record also supports **the mitigating factor of delay in the disciplinary proceedings.** *[Footnote 4: Respondent* **self-reported** *his June 30, 2000 suspension from the federal court on August 10, 2000; nevertheless,* **the ODC delayed filing formal charges for almost four years]**.

the mitigating factor of delay in the disciplinary proceedings [. . .] delayed filing formal charges for almost four years – Whose conduct is mitigated in a delay of years before charges are filed? The Justices are going to excuse the delay in their own interests. It is they who employ the disciplinary counsel, set the DC's budget, staff the office and instruct the DC as to the kind of matters the DC is going to pursue. All of this is either directly or indirectly under the Justices' control. Lawyers, unlike true professionals, are not in charge of their own ethical standards. That is a chore the judges have taken on – so as to exempt themselves from the application of such standards.

In August, 2000, I *self reported* my suspension by a federal court to three state Supreme Courts. I did so believing I owed a duty to the states, which had licensed me to practice law. Did I hold on to a hope that by so reporting, an inquiring beam of light might then be directed into the corners of this courthouse? Yes, I did, stupidly, think this.

Under all the circumstances, we find the sanction proposed by the disciplinary board is responsive to the misconduct and is consistent with our prior jurisprudence. Accordingly, we will suspend respondent from the practice of law for a period of three years, with all but eighteen months deferred, subject to the condition that any future misconduct may be grounds for making the deferred portion of the suspension executory or imposing additional discipline, as appropriate.

DECREE

Upon review of the findings and recommendations of the hearing committee and disciplinary board, and considering the record, it is ordered that Richard B. Cook, [IDD] Bar Roll number [IDD], be suspended from the practice of law for three years. It is further ordered that all but eighteen months of the suspension shall be deferred, subject to the condition that any future misconduct may be grounds for making the deferred portion of the suspension executory or for imposing additional discipline, as appropriate. All costs and expenses in the matter are assessed against respondent in accordance with Supreme Court Rule XIX, § 10.1, with legal interest to commence thirty days from the date of finality of this court's judgment until paid.

Is this a case of the canary in the mine or merely a personal catastrophe? The canary is dead. I know I will never have a law license again. I will never represent people who were so poor they could pay nothing for legal representation and had to pass the hat among immigrant relatives and friends if they were to pay me anything at all. Those people will now need a lawyer who not only will take their legal matter but have money left over to send the judge to Europe. *Buen viaje, Señor Juez! We await your return! And welcome your further orders!*

I will never recover any one of the three state law licenses I used to have because I am supposed to apologize and promise never to do this sort of thing again. I cannot control what the judges do, when confronted with misconduct by one of their own. I can control only what I do. What I will do is stay well away from a venue where one stuffs money into the semi-official spigot that flows under the courthouse. This is, I now know, part of the regular work of a lawyer. Another part of the attorney job description is to look the other way when I find out this has been going on.

CHAPTER VII

ORGAN GRINDER
v.
JOHANN SEBASTIAN
BACH

More than ninety-nine percent of all complaints about federal judges, made to supervising judges, are dismissed, without any investigation. From 1997-2006, 7,462 complaints against federal judges were filed; only seven were investigated; only nine judges were disciplined. These are complaints having to do with abuse of judicial power, bias, bribery, conflicts of interest, corruption, incompetence, mental disability, physical disability, and prejudice.

It is worth repeating: in this recent ten-year period, only seven out of seven thousand complaints made about judges were investigated. I did not know about this batting average when I complained about my judge during this period. In fairness to the judges, I have no doubt a lot of meritless complaints are filed. In fairness to me, seven investigations out of seven thousand filed complaints is discouraging data not readily available because a complaint, under controlling rules, is confidential and so is its virtually automatic dismissal.

You discover the Judicial Complaint batting average only by looking at the work of the Judicial Conference of the United States. Presided over by the Chief Justice of the Supreme Court, the Judicial Conference is the most powerful policy-making body in the Third Branch. This eminent body does not receive much media attention because the Judicial Conference, like the federal judiciary in general, makes its decisions in secret. Except for final orders and rulings from the bench, the inner operations of the Third Branch, dealing with such matters as time spent on the job, and court budgets, are hidden in an impenetrable thicket. Not even Indiana Jones could machete his way through, even if he hacked with the help of Bob, Rachel, Tommy Lee and all the rest of the Joneses.

Should we expect the Judicial Conference, appointed by the top judge, to train a shaft of light on the ethical standards theoretically imposed on judges in the federal judicial system? No, we should not. In essence, the Judicial Conference endorses the attitude of the supervising federal judges at the Circuit level. This means that, as in my complaints about my judge, you are made to become as inert as an organ grinder before J.S. Bach. *We are the geniuses of the inner sanctum; you belong out on the curb. We don't want to hear your little tune and or see the monkey dance!*

In response to a suggestion made in Congress a few years ago, the late Chief Justice William Rehnquist appointed Justice Stephen Breyer to chair a committee to report on the handling of complaints about judges. The committee's work led to the 2008 revision of the rules which govern complaints about judge misconduct, under the Judicial Conduct and Disability Act. Justice Breyer and his committee held few hearings and failed to publish (even in edited form) any of the complaints submitted to it. Yet the Committee concluded that the "vast majority" of the complaints filed about judicial misconduct were handled properly. We have to take the word of the committee that they did their semi-secret work properly and without themselves being implicated in any conflict of interest, such as a desire to keep the gift-to-the-judges spigot wide open.

Well, what about the substance of their work? Sadly, the revisions in the Judicial Complaint Rules reinforce the judicial privilege of simply dismissing complaints about judges without investigating them. In lieu of the new Rules, the judges who have approved them, could have published a simple statement on behalf of the federal judiciary: *We are as interested in the ethical conduct of federal judges as a moo cow is in the Kentucky Derby.*

These Rules reflect an important social compact, which is part of the blood and bone of our justice system: the judges pretend they are ethical and capable of self-regulation and the rest of us pretend we are too stupid to notice this is not the case. Examples of this compact are not hard to find in the revised Rules.

Revised Rule 2(b) authorizes the supervising Federal Circuit judges (who are mandated to receive complaints) simply to ignore any particular rule; thus *the Rules themselves are merely optional.* The hitter gets three strikes, unless the umpire decides the hitter should get four, or two. Or none at all.

Here is the text of Rule 2, and the official Commentary, with my **emphasis** added:

165

2. Effect and Construction

(a) Generally. These Rules are mandatory; they supersede any conflicting judicial council rules. Judicial councils may promulgate additional rules to implement the Act as long as those rules do not conflict with these Rules.

(b) Exception. **A Rule will not apply if**, when performing duties authorized by the Act, a chief judge, a special committee, a judicial council, the Judicial Conference Committee on Judicial Conduct and Disability, or the Judicial Conference of the United States expressly finds that **exceptional circumstances render application** of that Rule in a particular proceeding **manifestly unjust** or contrary to the purposes of the Act or these Rules.

Commentary on Rule 2

Unlike the Illustrative Rules, these Rules provide mandatory and nationally uniform provisions governing the substantive and procedural aspects of misconduct and disability proceedings under the Act. The mandatory nature of these Rules is authorized by 28 U.S.C. § 358(a) and (c). Judicial councils retain the power to promulgate rules consistent with these Rules. For example, a local rule may authorize the electronic distribution of materials pursuant to Rule 8(b).

Rule 2(b) recognizes that unforeseen and exceptional circumstances may call for a different approach in particular cases.

═══

The new Rule 2 demonstrates that the revised Rules actually loosen the already absurd looseness of the rules about judicial ethics. If *exceptional circumstances call for a different approach*, there are no written ethical rules. If you file a complaint against a federal judge, believing something might actually happen to the judge (and not to you, for filing it), you should repose a lesser degree of confidence in this belief than in the notion that Wotan is going to save you at the End Time. You might be right about the End Time but in the world of the Rules that govern Judicial Ethics, nothing is going to happen to a miscreant judge because nothing is supposed to happen.

There is more. Under the new definitions of misconduct (Rule 3 and its comments) we discover that the Code of Judicial Conduct is not binding on judges at all. For conduct that might get you a prison term if you bribed a politician, specific judge-created exemptions apply. The exemptions: (1) gifts by litigators and litigants to judges, (2) outside income for judges and (3) financial disclosure requirements of the judges. In each of these matters, there really is no rule at all.

Here is the definition of "misconduct" (from Rule 3), with my **emphasis** added, for purposes of discussion:

(h) Misconduct. Cognizable misconduct:

(1) is conduct prejudicial to the effective and expeditious administration of the business of the courts. Misconduct includes, but is not limited to:

A. using the judge's office to obtain special treatment for friends or relatives;
B. accepting bribes, gifts, or other personal favors related to the judicial office;
C. having improper discussions with parties or counsel for one side in a case;
D. treating litigants or attorneys in a demonstrably egregious and hostile manner;
E. engaging in partisan political activity or making inappropriately partisan statements;
F. soliciting funds for organizations; or
G. violating other specific, mandatory standards of judicial conduct, such as those pertaining to restrictions on outside income and requirements for financial disclosure.

(2) is conduct occurring outside the performance of official duties if the conduct might have a prejudicial effect on the administration of the business of the courts, including a substantial and widespread lowering of public confidence in the courts among reasonable people.

(3) **does not include:**
A. **an allegation that is directly related to the merits of a decision or procedural ruling.** An allegation that calls into question the correctness of a judge's ruling, including a failure to recuse, **without more**, is merits-related. **If the decision or ruling is alleged to be the result of an improper motive**, e.g., a bribe, ex parte contact, racial or ethnic bias, or improper conduct in rendering a decision or ruling, such as personally derogatory remarks irrelevant to the issues, the complaint **is not cognizable to the extent that it attacks the merits.**
B. an allegation about delay in rendering a decision or ruling, unless the allegation concerns an improper motive in delaying a particular decision or habitual delay in a significant number of unrelated cases.

======

Parts (1) and (2) offer to the public the prospect that a complaint about an unethical judge will be investigated. Part (3) takes away this prospect. Because misconduct *does not include an allegation that is directly related to the merits of a decision or procedural ruling. [. . .] If the decision or ruling is alleged to be the result of an improper motive [. . .] the complaint is not cognizable to the extent that it attacks the merits.* In other words, if you believe a judge has favored his friends by a ruling in their behalf, the ruling itself is NO EVIDENCE of favoritism.

169

In writing their own rules regulating their own conduct, the judges have given themselves impunity to accept bribes. If this approach were applied to any other agent subject to a bribe, it would be seen for the loophole it is. By the judges' logic, you cannot complain about a Department of Defense employee, who favored a contractor, if all the evidence you had was (1) the favorable DOD decision and (2) the contractor's gift to the employee. You could not complain about a mayor favoring a company leasing parking garages to the city, if your evidence was (1) the favorable contract and (2) the mayor on film, parking for free. You could not complain about a school principal in the business of providing school uniforms to the children in her school, if your evidence was (1) proof of the principal's ownership of the business plus (2) the decision by the school principal to use the principal's own business to provide the uniforms.

The official Commentary to Rule 3 emphasizes the "highly general" nature of the judicial code of conduct:

"the Code is in many potential applications aspirational rather than a set of disciplinary rules. Ultimately, the responsibility for determining what constitutes misconduct under the statute is the province of the judicial council of the circuit subject to such review and limitations as are ordained by the statute and by these Rules. Even where specific, mandatory rules exist -- for example, governing the receipt of gifts by judges, outside earned income, and financial disclosure obligations -- the distinction between the misconduct statute and the specific, mandatory

rules **must** be borne in mind. For example, an inadvertent, minor **violation of any one of these Rules**, promptly remedied when called to the attention of the judge, **might** still be a violation but **might not** rise to the level of misconduct under the statute. By contrast, **a pattern of such violations** of the Code **might** well rise to the level of misconduct."

A pattern of such conduct . . . might – Might means exactly the same thing as might not. This wiggly language is applied specifically to a pattern of misbehavior, such as "the receipt of gifts by judges, outside earned income, and financial disclosure obligations." Search the archives of the most autocratic regimes on earth and you will be pressed hard to find evidence of greater impunity to life-appointed arbiters of the conduct of everyone else. The judges could have taken their exalted, all-powerful positions as a charge to impose the highest standards of conduct upon themselves; they have done the opposite. An appointment to the federal judiciary is a ticket to ride.

If all this so far is not enough of a blanket exemption for unethical behavior, any judge who is mandated to at least accept a confidential complaint about another judge is under a second, decisive mandate. A supervising judge is actually ordered to let off an ethical outlier on the bench: the supervisor "must" keep in mind that "the Code is in many potential applications aspirational rather than a set of disciplinary rules." Judge Scooter aspired to avoid the bribe but he just couldn't do it.

The Code of Judicial Conduct is no more than a set of guidelines, not an enforceable mandate. The judges themselves wrote this stuff and apply it to themselves. A network of car thieves, writing their own Code of Car Thievery, could be schooled by the federal bench. The thieves code could then read:

*The law against car theft is applicable to all except ourselves, as we have decided to apply special rules to our own conduct, as follows: A theft of someone's automobile or a pattern of such thefts, might be inadvertent or might not rise to the level of actual misconduct, so as to violate our own special rules. The distinction between the rules we apply to our own thievery and the laws that apply to everyone else **must** be kept in mind. These rules need not apply in special circumstances, which we ourselves will identify in specific instances.*

Rule 8 requires that a complainant be identified and that the complaint be forwarded to the subject judge. You are not protected from the judge, should you file a confidential complaint, as I discovered to my professional destruction. (See chapters I-VI, above.)

Rule 11 (and also Rule 20) requires dismissal of a complaint "even if true" if the supervising judge (or the Judicial Council) determines that the judge's conduct "is not prejudicial to the effective and expeditious administration of the business of the courts and does not indicate a mental or physical disability resulting in inability to discharge the duties of judicial office." So long as gift giving to federal judges is kept secret, it is not "prejudicial." Anyway, an actual, favorable decision of the judge, in benefit of the gift giver, is not evidence of misconduct. See Rule 2.

Believe it or not, the likelihood of witness intimidation by the judge is cited as grounds for dismissing a complaint. I quote from the official comment (**emphasis** added):

"For example, a complaint alleges that an unnamed attorney told the complainant that the judge did X. The subject judge denies it. The **chief judge requests** that the complainant (who does not purport to have observed the judge do X) identify the unnamed witness, or that the unnamed witness come forward so that the chief judge can learn the unnamed witness's account. The complainant responds that he has spoken with the unnamed witness, that the unnamed witness is an attorney who practices in federal court, and that the unnamed **witness is unwilling to be identified** or to come forward. The allegation is then **properly dismissed** as containing allegations that are **incapable of being established through investigation.**"

unwilling to be identified - The complainant is not *compelled* to name the witness? The witness is not *compelled* to come forward? About a complaint dealing with: abuse of judicial power? Incompetence? Conflicts of interest? Mental disability? Bias? Bribery? Corruption? Prejudice? Physical disability? Confronted with a witness *unwilling to be identified*, the Chief Judge of a federal circuit – one step below the US Supreme Court – may *properly dismiss* the complaint. Why? It is deemed "incapable of being established through investigation." What *investigation*? There isn't one. Under these Rules, there is not supposed to be one.

Before you file your complaint against a federal judge (who gets a copy of your complaint), you now know that the supervising judge is not going to *demand* testimony or documents before dismissing your complaint. Hold off on filing your complaint against a federal judge, until you have shown this rule to your spouse or child or anyone dependent on your income as an attorney in federal court. 'Cause your income is going to go away.

A good argument could be made that a lawyer who files a complaint under these Rules, without the approval of every effected client, is committing malpractice. Read these rules to your corporate client before you file your confidential complaint. See if the client, who has put a $50,000 advance in your bank account, will leave the money there.

The commentary to Rule 11 specifies that even if "new and material evidence becomes available," an investigation need not be renewed if "at some point a renewed investigation may constitute harassment of the subject judge." It would be fun to hear a lawyer in a criminal matter try this argument out in court. *"Yes. Your Honor, I know there is new evidence against my client, but, Your Honor, the new evidence must not be admitted, Your Honor, because my client has reached the point where he is feeling harassed, Your Honor. . . . Your Honor?"*

On and on it goes in the new Code. Rule 13 and its commentary announce that any special committee that may be appointed to investigate a judicial complaint need **not** report a judge's criminal conduct to prosecutors or to grand juries. Don't take my word for it; here is the text of the relevant portion of Rule 13, with **emphasis** added.

(b) Criminal Conduct. If the committee's investigation concerns conduct that **may** be a crime, the committee must **consult** with the appropriate prosecutorial authorities to the extent permitted by the Act to avoid compromising any criminal investigation. The committee has final authority over the timing and extent of its investigation and the formulation of its recommendations.

Both states and the federal government prosecute government employees who take gifts from sources with whom they conduct official business. But a judge can accept gifts from attorneys and attorney associations – the very people with whom the judge conducts "official business." The *NY Times* recently reported (April 24, 2008, page C1) that an executive of a drug company has been indicted for "negotiating a secret pact" between his company and a generic drug maker "and then hiding the deal from federal regulators."A judge's meetings with litigators in social settings, with all costs covered by the litigators, are not characterized as *negotiations* or *secret pacts* and there are no prosecutors to worry about either as Rule 13(B) makes clear: regarding *"conduct that **may** be a crime, the committee must **consult** with the **appropriate** prosecutorial authorities."*
Since the Rules already declare (Rules 2 & 3, discussed above) that a litigator's gift to a judge is NOT bribery, this rule has limited application anyway. But even the faintest residue of pretended judicial concern for judicial malefaction is washed away by the actual words of the rule. Since "may"

means the same thing as "may not," there is little likelihood of any referrals to prosecutors.

In fact, there are not supposed to be any referrals. Rule 13 specifies that an investigative committee do no more than *consult* with prosecutors who, need to be *appropriate*. One can easily imagine this conclusion by judges who are colleagues of the subject of a complaint: *since the Chief Judge makes the initial determination about whether misconduct has occurred, this is a prosecutor's role, so let's just ask the Chief Judge about this and let it go at that.*

Neither the complainant nor the public will know about the decision not to refer evidence of judicial misconduct to an actual prosecutor. This is because the proceedings of an investigative committee are not likely ever to see the light of day, especially in the case of a dismissal of a judicial complaint, which happens over 99% of the time.

The final stopper is that no *consultation* with any outside prosecutorial authority can occur, except by majority vote of the committee. (See Rule 12(g).) All of the members of the committee are lifetime colleagues of Judge Skippy, who may be asked to return the favor, one day.

Rule 16 (e) takes up the sham of confidentiality before any investigative committee – and focuses particular aim at a complainant: *"In exercising its discretion under this Rule, a special committee may take into account the degree of **the complainant's** cooperation in preserving the confidentiality of the proceedings, including the identity of the subject judge."*

The attentive reader will recall that a judicial complaint which I filed was made public – by the subject judge. (See pages 32, 116.) This disclosure was a violation of the old Judicial Complaint Rules, though probably not a violation of the new and improved Rules.

In any case, the offending judge has no worries, because even a serious violation of these rules may be excused if the violation is characterized by the supervising judges as not "prejudicial to the effective and expeditious administration of the business of the courts." See Rule 11 or Rule 20 or what have you.

But counselor, what became of your confidential complaint? Well, it became evidence of professional misconduct – on my part. I quote from Formal Charges, which I have discussed earlier (page 37) and which were brought against me by a state Disciplinary Counsel: *"Your above detailed conduct constituting harassing and vexatious litigation* **centered around** *your January 19, 1999 Motion to Recuse Judge [IDD], the judge assigned to this case; and* **your complaint against Judge** *[IDD] which you filed with the U.S. Court of Appeals, [IDD] Circuit, on February 4, 1999, under docket Number [IDD]."*

The right, not to say the duty, to sound the alarm about undisputed misconduct by a United States District Judge is merely theoretical. When this right is exercised, your law license is placed at risk. Anxious to protect the judges against complaint, a state disciplinary counsel does not hesitate to compromise the most fundamental standard of honesty by neglecting to mention that my formal complaint was to have been held in confidence. So much for the integrity of both the judicial complaint apparatus, and the attorney disciplinary procedures; both have earned and are entitled to enjoy the same degree of prestige accorded to a state boxing commission.

The authors of the new Rules betray no indication that recent research in neuroscience has been taken into account. These studies show that even small gifts influence decision-making. *"When a gift or gesture of any size is bestowed, it imposes on the recipient a sense of indebtedness. The obligation to directly reciprocate, whether or not the recipient is conscious of it, tends to influence behavior. Feelings of obligation are not related to the size of the initial gift or favor."* Mere Science cannot be expected to slow down the rush to protect the judges' $$ spigot.

SOURCES:

The Revised Code is available from the Judicial Conference of the United States, as is the Breyer Committee Report, which is also at 239 F.R.D. 116 (Sept. 2006).

ABA Comments Regarding Draft Rules Governing Judicial Conduct and Disability Proceedings Undertaken Pursuant to 28 U.S.C. §§ 351-364

For a helpful critique of the new Code, see an "Open Letter" sent to each member of the Judicial Conference by Richard Cordero, Esq., available on the web at Judicial-Discipline-Reform.org.

recent research in neuroscience – quotation from Dana Katz, Arthur L. Caplan, and Jon F. Merz, *All Gifts Large and Small: Toward an Understanding of the Ethics of Pharmaceutical Industry Gift Giving*, <u>The American Journal of Bioethics</u> 3:3 (2003) 39-46.

CHAPTER VIII

I'M LYIN' I'M DYIN' DECLARATION

Is there a way through the thicket? Yes, there is. But there are a number of false solutions, that won't work. To save you some time, I will outline the bogus solutions and then point out the only real reformatory mechanism I know anything about.

JUDICIAL SELF-REGULATION:

This won't work. It has not worked up to now and there is no reason to think it will work in the future. The judges are just too addicted to gifts. They love to travel but don't want to pay for it, so they keep writing gift-excusing exceptions into their own codes of conduct. As demonstrated by the 2007-8 revisions to the Rules governing complaints of misconduct (see Chapter VII above) the lure of extra money into the pockets of the judges is just too enticing. They can't stop themselves.

Anyone who argues that self-regulation can guarantee ethical behavior by the judges should be willing to defer any consideration of salary increases for the judges until better rules than the "revised" ones are in place. The rules must include transparency as to all money going to members of the judiciary and from what sources. This requirement alone means the current rules must be scrapped.

REGULATION BY THE LEGAL PROFESSION:

This is a laugher. The lawyers are the ones who give the gifts, so naturally they have a big incentive to permit judges to accept gifts. The recently (2007) approved ABA Canon of Judicial Ethics explicitly permits gift giving to judges, as long as the gifts are called "wages" or "salaries" for such things as "speaking." And of course, the door is held wide open for the passing along of such emoluments as "honoraria, stipends, fees," and "other compensation."

The public alone ought to compensate full-time judges. This notion, though obvious, is as foreign to the scriveners as the theory of natural selection to a Kansas school board. Why would lawyer organizations ever turn off the spigot when attorneys are the ones stuffing money into one end of it?

CONGRESSIONAL OVERSIGHT:

This won't work. Even if there can be made a linkage between budget appropriations and the judicial complaint rules, you are dealing with two separate branches of government. No one wants Judge Scooter to have to come and explain himself in front of Representative Skippy. A Scooter-Skippy stand off will occasion more posturing than a beginner's Yoga class. Besides, Skippy is on the take more than Scooter is. Don't wait for a change in the law, if you are interested in genuine judicial ethics reform.

DENOUNCE THE JUDGE WHO IS ON THE TAKE:

This won't work. Unless you have an interest in the outcome of a particular lawsuit, you have no motivation to do this. So it won't get done. If you do have an interest in litigation, and publicly complain about the judge, you are going to lose your case. If you wait to complain until the lawsuit is over (and you lose), then you will discover that the rules currently in place do not recognize a judicial decision as evidence of misconduct; besides, everyone will think your complaint is sour grapes. Nothing will happen except this: you will have alienated all the judges who might hear your appeal.

SUE YOUR LAWYER FOR WHAT YOU FAILED TO RECOVER IN THE COURT OF THE MISCREANT JUDGE:

This is a variation on the idea of public finger-pointing that might actually help you – but without reforming the ethics of the judiciary. If, for the judges, it is all about extra money, than that is what your lawsuit is about, too. So, do you care who pays you? Money from your lawyer's malpractice insurer is just as good as money from the opposing party.

After your lawsuit has been filed, ask your lawyer to tell you what he/she knows about the ethics of your judge. If the lawyer knows nothing, then ask the lawyer to find out and to report back to you. The lawyer is likely to come back with something about the judge – with these examples taken from actual judicial practice:

- the judge has taken big campaign contributions from your opposing counsel;
- the judge (or a close family member) owns a building with lawyers as renters;
- the judge takes trips paid for by opposing counsel through an attorney association;
- the judge has been accepting payouts for years from his former law firm, whose partners do business in his court;
- the judge's spouse is in some kind of business with lawyers in town;
- the judge has a drinking/gambling/drug problem, and this is notoriously well known around the courthouse;
- the judge has installed a stripper's pole in his chambers, the better to be entertained by a clerk with whom he is having an affair;
- the judge has had an affair with a lawyer in the firm of opposing counsel;
- the judge is having an affair with a person the judge has sentenced to prison;
- the judge does not report all income on the required financial disclosure forms;
- the judge sometimes orders civil defendants to pay money to charities selected by the judge;
- Etc.

Armed with this information, ask your attorney to file a confidential complaint. If your lawyer declines to do so, and even gives you good reasons for refusing (such as the dangerous absurdity of the judicial complaint rules), then, if you lose your case, sue your lawyer for not protecting you against an unethical judge, whom the lawyer knew was bad news. All the stuff you learned about the judge might come out and you might then turn your defeat in court into a win around the settlement table with your former lawyer. It would be interesting to hear a lawyer's defense for failing to file a complaint about judicial misconduct, after a client requested that one be filed: the particular bad conduct is not covered by the ethics rules; the Canons of Judicial Ethics are pointless; the Judicial Complaint Rules are useless; and so on.

This advice is not offered seriously because it is unlikely to make the judges behave. There is one solution that *will* make them behave. We shall call this a commitment to best practices, or the:

I'M LYING I'M DYING DECLARATION

The following statement should become part of any application for appointment to the bench, state or federal, and should be solicited as a routine requirement before an appointment is made. A nominee's signature on this declaration ought to be a condition for service as a judge. A few modifications to this statement would make it useful in state court systems. This BEST PRACTICES DECLARATION has the great merit of being capable of implementation without dependence upon a change in the law or upon agreement by the apparatus of the judiciary or by an amendment to the existing canons or codes of ethics. It would be something required of new judges.

You can get this change made by asking – no, insisting – that this declaration be signed by anyone who is nominated or is seeking election to a judgeship. There could be little in the way of objection since this pledge is merely an affirmation that an individual who wants to be a judge is willing to forgo gifts.

DECLARATION OF BEST PRACTICES

"I declare under penalty of perjury that, except in the case of a close relative, I have never given any money or gift or any item of value to a judge, either personally or through any business, entity, or partnership or through any association of which I am a member.

"I further declare that, except for my salary and any other money or benefits forwarded to me from funds properly appropriated to and allocated by the judicial entity which employs me, I will not accept any gift or benefit or any item of any value whatsoever from any entity or organization whatsoever or from any person, except a close relative, during my service as a judge.

"Should any such just-described prohibited gift or benefit be accepted by me and discovered subsequent to my successful accession to the judicial position under present consideration for me, I shall immediately resign my judicial post and I shall neither resist any formal efforts to remove me, nor will I seek or accept any subsequent judicial appointment or service."

A supplement to this Declaration would be a policy which requires every decision, decree, ruling or order in every court to contain this preface:

> The undersigned judicial officer affirms that neither the officer nor any member of the officer's immediate family has had and none presently has any financial connection to any of the litigants or litigators who are parties to or who have made an appearance in this matter.

Good Luck.

"A long habit of not thinking a thing wrong gives it a superficial appearance of being right."

Thomas Paine

Common Sense

(1776)

CONCLUSION

Every lawyer should be under a mandate to report obvious misconduct by a judge. In my case, I discovered and reported misconduct which had to do with a travel gift to a judge which was followed by a decision (permitting an amended complaint) which greatly benefitted a gift giver and which was effected by the judge contravening the rules of the judge's own court. This is exactly the kind of shenanigans that ought to be sanctioned. Unfortunately, the opposite is true. The judge-written rules enthusiastically permit this kind of thing. Likewise, there must be neither threat nor reprisal directed at an attorney for coming forward. Unfortunately, this is exactly what happens. It happened to me.

A perpetual judgment that you are an unethical person is not a minor kerfuffle in one's life. It is a curtailment of many actual and potential opportunities both for income and for service. It is the death of your public self. If *the first night is the worst thing about death* (Juan Ramón Jiménez) you wake up to this rot and molder every morning.

Statements made to a judge concerning his own misconduct must never again become the basis for disciplinary action – if the statements are true. Throwing away the career and the public life of an honest attorney – by judges who refuse to admit

187

that he was complaining truthfully about the misconduct of one of their own – is a cynical farce, a shameful caricature of a proper judicial proceeding. I was turned out of the legal profession without any specific finding of dishonesty, fraud, deceit or misrepresentation; it was enough that I had filed a confidential complaint and, in pleadings, pointed to specific, documented instances of improper conduct.

The state Supreme Court Justices who condemned me publicly – and the Disciplinary Counsel in their employ – decided that the conduct of a federal judge would not be scrutinized. In their rush to send a warning to the bar, they, like Parsee, Ahab's pilot, have shattered the ship's quadrant (*Moby Dick*, Ch CXVIII). Guided now only by their appetites (Aristotle's *appetitions*), they may catch and kill their pray, but at the risk of the ship and all hands. By their unfortunate act, the Justices have left themselves and the honest lawyers in their courts no safe channel through the mire of gifts to judges and the return favors, offered up by judges to their benefactors. *Mal de todos, consuelo de tontos:* only the foolish find consolation in an evil that is injurious to all.

The Justices put my disciplinary proceedings into the hands of lawyers who were members of the very organization I had complained about, and who were in practice before the miscreant judge. The Justices winked at this travesty in the disciplinary system they supervise.

Any professional regulatory authority empowered to deprive its members of their reputation and their ability to earn an income should be subject to the highest standards of objectivity and fairness. In the legal community, the

188

opposite is the norm. The rules which govern the behavior of lawyers are explicitly intended to overlook complaints about the venal and self-interested behavior of the most powerful members of the profession. The judges make the rules and see to their own insulation from criticism, oversight and transparency in their dealings with persons interested in judicial outcomes. The judges take pains to block any examination of their off-the-books income streams. Anyone who is so incautious as to rely on the prescribed complaint rules and who comes forward, confidentially, to object to obvious instances of be-robed venality can expect to be subjected to the severest sanction.

The solution to this mess lies with the judicial selection process, not with sitting judges. When it comes to judicial standards of ethics, the incumbent judges are useless. They are enriched by the existing ethical canons and judicial complaint rules. These rules are designed to protect judicial misconduct. The current canons and rules ought to be an embarrassment to everybody. Identifying judicial misconduct to the solons themselves is like feeding grease to a duck. The content will pass through the system and leave not a trace, except a smelly little puddle that everyone will go out of their way to step around.

Any person who aspires to the bench should be held to a higher standard than the *money-to-me/ruling-for-you* two-step. Prospective judges must be made to foreswear the taking of gifts. Period. Any who decline to do so should not be placed on the bench.

They have mouths but they speak not.

Eyes have they, but they see not.

They have ears, but they hear not.

Noses have they, but they smell not.

They have hands but they handle not.

Feet have they, but they walk not.

Neither speak they through their

throat.

PSALMS 115: 5-7

INDEX

SUPREME COURT OF LOUISIANA

NO. 06-B-0426

IN RE: RICHARD B. COOK

ATTORNEY DISCIPLINARY PROCEEDINGS

PER CURIAM

This disciplinary matter arises from formal charges filed by the Office of Disciplinary Counsel ("ODC") against respondent, Richard B. Cook, an attorney licensed to practice law in Louisiana.

UNDERLYING FACTS

In November 1996, respondent began representing the plaintiffs in a civil matter captioned *Evelyn Faye Allen, et al. v. Richard Stalder, et al.*, No. 95-1118 on the docket of the United States District Court for the Western District of Louisiana, Alexandria Division, Judge F. A. Little, Jr. presiding (hereinafter referred to as "*Allen*"). The plaintiffs in *Allen* were a group of female prison inmates who alleged their civil rights were violated as a result of physical and sexual abuse at the hands of their prison guards.

On June 26, 1998, respondent filed a motion in *Allen* in which he implied that the court had improperly never "permitted representative civil rights plaintiffs to proceed as class representatives." He also implied that Judge Little had improperly met with and dissuaded a local attorney from enrolling as co-counsel for the plaintiffs.

On December 31, 1998, respondent filed a motion entitled "Plaintiff's Response to the State Defendants' Motion to Dismiss Certain Plaintiffs." In this motion, respondent stated that if Judge Little granted the defendants' motion, then "the courts in the Western District of Louisiana can be reserved almost entirely for wealthy (predominantly white) litigants, and courts and counsel need not be concerned with poor (predominantly black) plaintiffs." He also claimed that Judge Little compounded the "lack of balance" between the plaintiffs' resources and the defendants' resources through his "unwritten orders, his failure to respond to plaintiff motions, [and] his refusal to even place this case on the docket for many months at the outset." Finally, respondent suggested that this case would not end until "either the plaintiffs prevail or the Court concludes that the rape and abuse of inmates by their guards is perfectly OK."

On January 11, 1999, respondent filed a motion in which he requested that the following subjects be discussed at a status conference: 1) the delay in placing the *Allen* case on the docket; 2) reconsideration of the denial of the plaintiffs' class representation; 3) the failure of the court to place one of the plaintiffs' motions on the docket; 4) whether the court has ever authorized class representation in civil rights claims; 5) whether there is a consensus in the court to never allow these types of cases to go forward with class representatives; 6) why Judge Little's unwritten orders have never been put in writing; 7) whether Judge Little met with a local attorney and dissuaded him from enrolling as co-counsel for the plaintiffs; 8) whether Judge Little has ever appointed counsel to represent an incarcerated person who has complained about conditions of confinement; and 9) whether the court as a whole has ever allowed such a plaintiff to get beyond a defendant's summary judgment or other motion dismissing the complaint.

2

On January 14, 1999, respondent filed a motion to recuse Judge Little. The basis for his motion was his belief that his clients' opportunity for a fair trial was "slipping away" due to Judge Little's conduct in the *Allen* case as well as in the case of *Vergie Lee Valley v. Rapides Parish School Board*, No. 96-30441 on the docket of the United States District Court for the Western District of Louisiana, Alexandria Division (hereinafter referred to as "*Valley*"). Respondent alleged that one of the attorneys in the *Valley* case was Judge Little's former law partner and the president of an organization that paid for the judge's overseas trip to speak at its conference while the *Valley* case was pending before him. Thereafter, the case was settled in favor of this attorney's client. As such, respondent alleged that "the judge permitted this counsel's client to benefit from his judicial function." Furthermore, because of the judge's alleged conduct in *Valley*, respondent argued that the judge "has not maintained the necessary firewall between his personal and his judicial relations and ought not hear Constitutional matters." Regarding the judge's conduct in *Allen*, respondent argued that he acted improperly in denying the plaintiffs' motion for class representation without conducting a hearing, failed to notice one of the plaintiffs' motions for a hearing, and twice issued oral orders without later putting them in writing. Respondent also accused Judge Little of engaging in "lax case management" and having an "indifference to propriety." He also argued that Judge Little "has not met the judicial requirement of an avoidance of impropriety and the appearance of bias and partiality." Based on these reasons, respondent argued Judge Little should be recused. Judge Little denied the motion to recuse on January 20, 1999, stating that respondent included only vague allegations that did not identify a conflict the judge has with the *Allen* case.

Respondent also filed a complaint against Judge Little with the United States Court of Appeals for the Fifth Circuit based on the *Valley* allegations in his motion to recuse. The Fifth Circuit dismissed the complaint on February 2, 1999, stating "[b]ecause Judge Little was not acting improperly either in presiding over a suit in which his former partner appeared as counsel, or in attending the conference, Judge Little is not subject to discipline for the combination of the two."

On February 10, 1999, Judge Little provided detailed reasons for his denial of respondent's motion to recuse. Essentially, Judge Little ruled that the motion to recuse was frivolous and cited the Fifth Circuit's dismissal of respondent's judicial complaint in support of the denial of the motion.

On February 22, 1999, respondent filed a second complaint against Judge Little with the Fifth Circuit based on Judge Little's reference to the Fifth Circuit's dismissal of respondent's first judicial complaint, thereby publishing the fact that respondent was a judicial complainant. The complaint was also based on an allegation that Judge Little had a financial interest in the building housing his former law firm, one of whose partners was representing a party in a case before Judge Little. The Fifth Circuit dismissed this complaint on May 12, 1999.

In April 1999, respondent filed a second motion to recuse Judge Little in the *Allen* case. The motion was based on Judge Little making public the fact that respondent had filed a judicial complaint against him with the Fifth Circuit. Judge Little denied the motion on May 6, 1999.

Thereafter, in an attempt to further investigate his allegations regarding Judge Little's improprieties in other cases, including the *Valley* case, respondent sought to take the deposition of Jan Holloway, the former office manager of Judge Little's former law firm, Gold, Weems, Bruser, Sues & Rundell ("Gold"), and its real estate partner, 2001 Odyssey Partnership ("Odyssey"). However, neither Gold nor Odyssey were parties to the *Allen* case; thus, Judge Little quashed the deposition. Respondent also sought to subpoena documents from Gold and Odyssey. Both filed objections to the subpoenas, and United States Magistrate Judge James Kirk, the presiding

magistrate in the *Allen* case, quashed the subpoenas in a ruling dated July 28, 1999.

Moreover, Magistrate Judge Kirk indicated that respondent "persists in what can only

be described now as a pattern of harassment in an attempt to influence the district

judge."

On February 3, 2000, Judge Little assigned the *Allen* case to Magistrate Judge

Kirk for pretrial preparation. In response, respondent filed a motion to reconsider the

assignment to Magistrate Judge Kirk, raising the same arguments as raised in the two

motions to recuse and the two judicial complaints against Judge Little. Specifically,

respondent stated,

> the plaintiffs are unwilling to litigate their legal interests
> before a Court who has received a valuable gratuity from
> litigators with matters pending in his court. The plaintiffs
> are also concerned about the Court's fairness, because the
> Court has improperly published a Judicial Complaint and
> has identified their counsel as Complainant, thus
> manifesting an inclination to seek to humiliate and coerce
> their counsel.

Respondent then indicated he may "seek extra-judicial supervision to enforce the

appropriate canons of behavior" because the Fifth Circuit was "unable or unwilling

to supervise the district judges as to ethical matters." Judge Little denied the motion

to reconsider on February 28, 2000.

On April 4, 2000, after Judge Little and Magistrate Judge Kirk suggested that

respondent's conduct may warrant sanctions, respondent filed a motion seeking a

hearing on sanctions. In the motion, respondent reurged his request that Judge Little

be recused. He also claimed that Judge Little improperly quashed Ms. Holloway's

deposition and reurged his request to depose her. The motion was referred to

Magistrate Judge Kirk, who found the following:

> In this case, it appears that plaintiff's attorney's continued
> attacks are calculated to provoke the district judge in an

> effort toward forum shopping. Cook's attacks appear to be
> an attempt to influence the result of this case by threats,
> intimidation and harassment of the district judge.
> Warnings by the district judge and by the undersigned have
> not corrected Cook's behavior.

Accordingly, Magistrate Judge Kirk ordered that respondent be referred to Judge

Little for consideration of contempt proceedings, sanctions, and/or referral to the

Louisiana Attorney Disciplinary Board. He also ordered that the clerk of court stop

accepting from respondent any pleadings concerning matters raised in the motions to

recuse or concerning Ms. Holloway's deposition. Finally, he ordered respondent to

learn the Louisiana Rules of Professional Conduct, the Code of Professionalism, and

the Code of Professionalism in the Courts adopted by the Louisiana Supreme Court

and comply with same in his activities in and pleadings submitted to the United States

District Court, Western District of Louisiana, Alexandria Division.

On May 31, 2000, Judge Little issued an order adopting Magistrate Judge

Kirk's ruling and ordered respondent to show cause why he should not be sanctioned.

Judge Little sanctioned respondent on June 30, 2000, ordering him to pay $7,500 to

the clerk of court and suspending him from practice before the court until he paid the

fine. Respondent paid the fine in August 2000.

Between October 25, 2000 and March 6, 2001, respondent was ordered three

times to show cause why he should not be sanctioned for subsequent failures to

comply with deadlines and court orders, including orders to cease raising the same

issues for which he was previously sanctioned. Pursuant to those show cause orders,

respondent was ordered to pay $1,243.75 and $1,621.75 in attorney's fees to the

defendants on February 22, 2001, fined $2,000 on February 22, 2001, and fined

$4,000 on February 26, 2001.

Also on February 26, 2001, respondent filed a motion to recuse Magistrate

Judge Kirk, citing his April 25, 2000 order that respondent not interview an inmate incarcerated in Avoyelles Parish, which order respondent claimed was punishment for having filed a judicial complaint against Judge Little. Magistrate Judge Kirk denied the motion.

Respondent paid the attorney's fees, the $2,000 fine, and the $4,000 fine in March 2001. On March 26, 2001, he filed a pleading in which he apologized to the court, explaining that he recognizes his conduct went "beyond the permissible limits of advocacy." Respondent also filed, under seal, a motion to withdraw as counsel of record for the *Allen* plaintiffs. Respondent was dismissed as counsel on May 10, 2001.

DISCIPLINARY PROCEEDINGS

Formal Charges

On April 28, 2004, the ODC filed one count of formal charges against respondent, alleging that his conduct violated Rules 3.1 (meritorious claims and contentions), 4.4 (respect for the rights of third persons), 8.4(a) (violation of the Rules of Professional Conduct), and 8.4(d) (engaging in conduct prejudicial to the administration of justice) of the Rules of Professional Conduct. Respondent answered the formal charges, essentially denying the allegations of misconduct.[1]

Formal Hearing

This matter proceeded to a formal hearing on the merits. Respondent participated in the hearing via telephone.

---

[1] In his answer, respondent continued to insist that Judge Little engaged in misconduct. Therefore, because his allegations of misconduct against Judge Little were truthful, respondent argued that he himself did not engage in any misconduct.

Both respondent and the ODC introduced documentary evidence at the hearing. The ODC called Patricia Bowers (defense counsel in the *Allen* case),[2] Magistrate Judge Kirk, and Rodney Rabalais (defense counsel in the *Allen* case)[3] to testify before the committee. Respondent did not testify on his own behalf, nor did the ODC call him to testify.

Hearing Committee Recommendation

After considering this matter, the hearing committee made factual findings as follows:

The first sign of trouble in the *Allen* case appeared on June 26, 1998 when respondent filed a pleading in which he moved the court to "investigate its own docket and determine whether this Court has ever permitted representative civil rights plaintiffs to proceed as class representatives." In the same pleading, respondent implied that Judge Little had engaged in efforts to dissuade an attorney from enrolling as co-counsel for the plaintiffs. Respondent made similar insinuations in his response to a court order dated December 30, 1998.

Respondent then filed a motion to recuse Judge Little, accusing him of partiality in favor of a litigant's attorney who was a member of Judge Little's former law firm and, as president of a legal association, arranged for Judge Little to travel

---

[2] Ms. Bowers testified that respondent engaged in "almost constant warfare with the judge" during the case. Respondent also filed redundant pleadings, raising the same issues over and over again, which had to be responded to and ruled on each time, making the case go on longer than normal. Since she billed by the hour, respondent's redundant pleadings caused her to bill her clients two to three times more in attorney's fees than normal. While she felt that respondent had the "best of intentions," she also felt he "stepped over the line," was "misguided," and "got carried away about the judge."

[3] Mr. Rabalais testified that respondent filed redundant pleadings and began to focus more on Judge Little, making "outlandish" accusations against the judge, which diverted time and attention away from the merits of the case. Mr. Rabalais also testified that he had to bill his clients for the time he spent on the redundant issues. Finally, he testified that the case was concluded approximately six months after respondent was dismissed.

to Italy to address the association's meeting. The motion was denied, and in reasons for denying the motion, Judge Little referred to the fact that respondent filed a judicial complaint against him. Respondent then filed another motion to recuse, alleging that Judge Little violated Rule 15 of the Fifth Circuit's Rules Governing Complaints of Judicial Misconduct or Disability, which mandates that judicial complaints remain confidential.

Judge Little's relationship with the aforementioned attorney became a topic of intense scrutiny for respondent. On June 29, 1999, Gold objected to respondent's subpoena for the following records: checks made payable to Judge Little from 1984 to the present; checks made payable to Judge Little's wife from 1984 to present; and checks made payable to any party, which might benefit Judge Little, his wife, or any of his relatives. Odyssey objected to an identical subpoena. On July 28, 1999, Magistrate Judge Kirk ruled that the requested records in the subpoenas were irrelevant and the subpoenas themselves were harassing.

On July 13, 1999, respondent filed a request that the above objections be transferred to another court for consideration. On July 16, 1999, respondent deposed Ms. Holloway, questioning her about the same matters that were the subjects of the above subpoenas. However, Ms. Holloway's attorney objected to the taking of the deposition and instructed her not to answer. Thus, during the deposition, the parties called Judge Little to resolve the issue, and Judge Little disallowed any questioning of Ms. Holloway.

In response to Judge Little's February 3, 2000 order assigning the *Allen* case to Magistrate Judge Kirk for pretrial preparation, respondent filed a request to refer the case to another district court because the plaintiffs did not want to litigate their issues before a judge who "received a valuable gratuity from litigators with matters pending in his court" and who "improperly published a Judicial Complaint and has identified their counsel as a Complainant, thus manifesting an inclination to seek to humiliate and coerce their counsel."

In response to respondent's motions to recuse Judge Little, Magistrate Judge Kirk suggested that their frivolous nature might lead to sanctions. The court did not order sanctions or order respondent to show cause why he should not be sanctioned. However, on his own motion, respondent sought a hearing on sanctions, taking this opportunity to also reiterate his allegations of misconduct against Judge Little and his request to depose Ms. Holloway. In response, Magistrate Judge Kirk listed twenty-eight incidents of respondent's behavior he felt warranted sanctions. Respondent reacted to this ruling by reiterating his previous allegations against Judge Little.

Respondent never appealed the denial of his clients' motions to recuse. Instead, he continued to reiterate his allegations against Judge Little and later added allegations against Magistrate Judge Kirk. He also continued to raise the issue of deposing Ms. Holloway. His allegations of misconduct against Judge Little continued up to and including the formal hearing in this matter.

Based on these findings, the hearing committee determined that respondent violated Rules 3.1, 4.4, and 8.4(d) of the Rules of Professional Conduct. Respondent did not pursue the proper review of Judge Little's rulings through interlocutory appeal. Instead, he continued to pursue the same issues to the point of obsession and in a vexatious manner. Furthermore, despite having notice that Gold and Odyssey, who were not parties to the *Allen* suit, objected to his subpoenas, respondent attempted to obtain the information through Ms. Holloway's deposition. Respondent's conduct as a whole amounted to conduct prejudicial to the administration of justice.

The committee determined that respondent knowingly engaged in disruptive conduct in the *Allen* case. However, his behavior was not intended to personally benefit himself or his clients. The committee agreed with Ms. Bowers, who felt that respondent believed what he was doing was right but allowed his cause to become a crusade. In mitigation, the committee also placed significant weight on a report of respondent's psychotherapist, who indicated that respondent's response to perceived injustices resulted in obsessive behavior, which opinion is consistent with the evidence in the record.

Under these circumstances, the committee recommended that respondent be suspended for three years.

Neither respondent nor the ODC filed an objection to the hearing committee's recommendation.

Disciplinary Board Recommendation

After reviewing this matter, the disciplinary board determined that the hearing committee's findings of fact are not manifestly erroneous. The board also determined that respondent violated the Rules of Professional Conduct as alleged in the formal charges. Specifically, the board found that instead of proceeding with interlocutory appeal of the denial of the motion to recuse, respondent continued to "tirelessly" pursue the issue at the district court level without a good faith legal basis to do so. Furthermore, respondent's pursuit of discovery from third persons not involved in the *Allen* case was burdensome to these parties. Respondent's conduct caused undue expense and effort in the federal court proceedings and also caused the defendants to accrue extra expenses.

Based on these findings, the board determined that respondent knowingly, if not intentionally, violated a duty owed to the legal system, causing significant harm to the federal courts as well as Gold, Odyssey, and the defendants in the *Allen* case.

Relying on the ABA's *Standards for Imposing Lawyer Sanctions*, the board determined that the baseline sanction is a period of suspension.

As aggravating factors, the board identified a pattern of misconduct and refusal to acknowledge the wrongful nature of the conduct. As mitigating factors, it found the absence of a prior disciplinary record, personal or emotional problems, full and free disclosure to the disciplinary board and a cooperative attitude toward the proceedings, inexperience in the practice of law (admitted 1992), and imposition of other penalties or sanctions.

Turning to the issue of an appropriate sanction, the board looked to this court's prior jurisprudence and determined that the three-year suspension recommended by the hearing committee is too harsh. Like the attorneys in *In re: Zohdy*, 04-2361 (La. 1/19/05), 892 So. 2d 1277; *In re: Stratton*, 03-3198 (La. 4/2/04), 869 So. 2d 794; and *In re: Boydell*, 00-0086 (La. 5/26/00), 760 So. 2d 326, respondent filed repetitive and unwarranted pleadings in ongoing litigation. Also, like *Stratton*, respondent's frivolous and harassing claims and requests for discovery burdened third persons. However, the board found that respondent's conduct and the resulting harm were not as egregious as that found in the three cited cases. Furthermore, respondent's conduct spanned approximately three years, which was considerably less than the ten-year spans in *Boydell* and *Stratton*. Respondent also did not cause direct harm to his clients as did *Zohdy* and *Boydell*. Taking these circumstances into account, as well as the numerous mitigating factors present, the board determined that it is appropriate to defer eighteen months of a three-year suspension.

Accordingly, the board recommended that respondent be suspended from the practice of law for three years, with all but eighteen months deferred.

Neither respondent nor the ODC filed an objection to the disciplinary board's recommendation.

DISCUSSION

Bar disciplinary matters come within the original jurisdiction of this court. La. Const. art. V, § 5(B). Consequently, we act as triers of fact and conduct an independent review of the record to determine whether the alleged misconduct has been proven by clear and convincing evidence. *In re: Quaid*, 94-1316 (La. 11/30/94), 646 So. 2d 343; *Louisiana State Bar Ass'n v. Boutall*, 597 So. 2d 444 (La. 1992). While we are not bound in any way by the findings and recommendations of the hearing committee and disciplinary board, we have held the manifest error standard is applicable to the committee's factual findings. *See In re: Caulfield*, 96-1401 (La. 11/25/96), 683 So. 2d 714; *In re: Pardue*, 93-2865 (La. 3/11/94), 633 So. 2d 150.

We find the record supports the hearing committee's factual findings, and that respondent violated the Rules of Professional Conduct as alleged in the formal charges. Respondent filed repetitive and unwarranted pleadings in ongoing litigation. He also made frivolous and harassing claims for discovery against third persons not involved in the litigation.

Having found evidence of professional misconduct, we now turn to a determination of the appropriate sanction for respondent's actions. In considering that issue, we are mindful that disciplinary proceedings are designed to maintain high standards of conduct, protect the public, preserve the integrity of the profession, and deter future misconduct. *Louisiana State Bar Ass'n v. Reis*, 513 So. 2d 1173 (La. 1987). The discipline to be imposed depends upon the facts of each case and the seriousness of the offenses involved considered in light of any aggravating and mitigating circumstances. *Louisiana State Bar Ass'n v. Whittington*, 459 So. 2d 520 (La. 1984).

Respondent knowingly violated a duty owed to the legal system, causing significant harm to the federal courts as well as others. The baseline sanction for this misconduct is suspension.

The aggravating and mitigating factors found by the board are supported by the record. The record also supports the mitigating factor of delay in the disciplinary proceedings.[4] Under all the circumstances, we find the sanction proposed by the disciplinary board is responsive to the misconduct and is consistent with our prior jurisprudence.

Accordingly, we will suspend respondent from the practice of law for a period of three years, with all but eighteen months deferred, subject to the condition that any future misconduct may be grounds for making the deferred portion of the suspension executory or imposing additional discipline, as appropriate.

DECREE

Upon review of the findings and recommendations of the hearing committee and disciplinary board, and considering the record, it is ordered that Richard B. Cook, Louisiana Bar Roll number 21248, be suspended from the practice of law for three years. It is further ordered that all but eighteen months of the suspension shall be deferred, subject to the condition that any future misconduct may be grounds for making the deferred portion of the suspension executory or for imposing additional discipline, as appropriate. All costs and expenses in the matter are assessed against respondent in accordance with Supreme Court Rule XIX, § 10.1, with legal interest to commence thirty days from the date of finality of this court's judgment until paid.

---

[4] Respondent self-reported his June 30, 2000 suspension from the federal court on August 10, 2000; nevertheless, the ODC delayed filing formal charges for almost four years.